THE FIVE
Lives
OF THE
Kentucky River

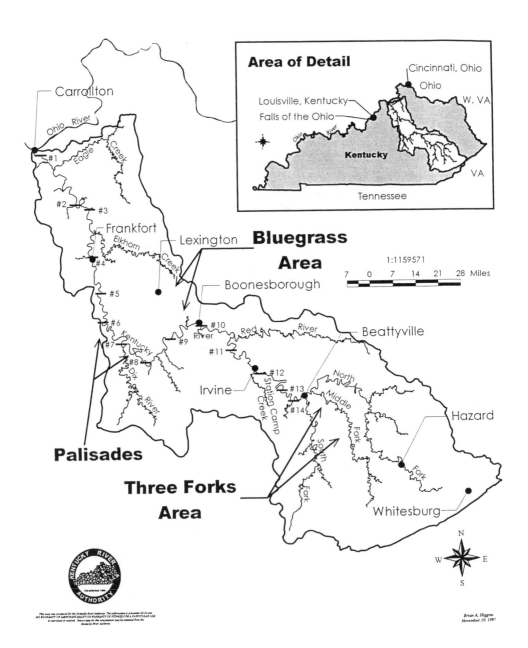

Area of Detail

Cincinnati, Ohio
Ohio
W. VA
Louisville, Kentucky
Falls of the Ohio
Ohio River
Kentucky
VA
Tennessee

Carrollton

Ohio River

#1

Eagle Creek

#2 #3

Frankfort

Elkhorn Creek

Lexington

Bluegrass Area

#4

#5

Boonesborough

1:1159571

7 0 7 14 21 28 Miles

#6

Kentucky River

Red River

Beattyville

#7

#9 #10 River

#8

Dix River

#11

#12

Station Camp Creek

North Fork

Hazard

Irvine

#13

Middle Fork

#14

Palisades

South Fork

Fork

Three Forks Area

Whitesburg

N
W E
S

KENTUCKY RIVER AUTHORITY
Established 1986

This map was produced for the Kentucky River Authority. The information is presented AS IS and
NO WARRANTY OF MERCHANTABILITY OR WARRANTY OF FITNESS FOR A PARTICULAR USE
is expressed or implied. Source data for this compilation may be obtained from the
Kentucky River Authority.

Brian A. Higgins
November 10, 1997

THE FIVE
Lives
OF THE
Kentucky River

by
William F. Grier

Jesse Stuart Foundation
Ashland, Kentucky
2001

Library of Congress Cataloging-in-Publication Data

Grier, William F., 1932-
    The Five Lives of the Kentucky River / by William F. Grier.
        p. cm.
    Summary: Views the history of the Kentucky River as five separate lives: "Prehistoric to the Late 1780s," "Flatboats and Keelboats to the Dawn of Steam, 1780s to 1842," "The Golden Age of Locks and Dams, 1842-1932," "Decay and Decline, 1931-1986," and "The River Reborn, 1986 Onward."
    ISBN 0-945084-92-7

        1. Kentucky River (Ky.)--History--Juvenile literature. 2. Kentucky River (Ky.)--History--Pictorial works--Juvenile literature. [1. Kentucky River (Ky.)--History.] I. Title.

F457.K3 G75 2001
976.9'3--dc21

                                                                2001038200

Published by:
Jesse Stuart Foundation
P.O. Box 669 • Ashland, Ky 41105
2001

CONTENTS

Introduction

Introduction

A river is a living creature. It has personality, feelings, moods, and its own life. The Kentucky River is no exception; at times it rages, at times its flow is a smooth purr, and at times it withdraws into itself like a wrinkled old man. Its life begins in the steep, turbulent coal fields of Eastern Kentucky with tributary names like Hell's Creek, Hell-for-Certain Creek, Troublesome Creek, and Quicksand Creek. Mid-life is spent in the rich, Bluegrass region of Kentucky, where it drains the hoofprints of Derby winners and where the rhythm of Shaker meetings once wafted across its water. Highbridge, which was built as the *"highest bridge over a navigable waterway in America,"* spans the River near its midsection at the sheer cliffs on both sides known as the Palisades. Hard by the Palisades is the Valley View ferry, in operation since 1785 and the oldest continuously operated business in Kentucky and probably west of the Appalachian mountains. Before sinking into the Ohio River downstream from Cincinnati, the River is bent and burdened, and the shoreline hides the vine-covered buildings of a long-abandoned summer resort where aching bodies once sought the soothing powers of its bubbling springs and lovers walked hand in hand along secluded shoreline paths.

The Kentucky River has known five lives, each distinct yet overlapping, with each life built upon the one that came before. Kentucky is watered by many rivers—the Green, the Licking, the Big

Sandy, the Salt, the Barren, and many others—but none wields the grip upon Kentuckians that the Kentucky River does. The name, of course, ties it to its sons and daughters, but there is much more than this relationship. First, the river was the pathway of the earliest settlers into the heartland west of the Appalachian mountains. Settlers came both up the River and down it to reach the fertile bluegrass area which was and is the spiritual dwelling of blueblood Kentuckians. History has dwelt largely upon those who followed Daniel Boone and Col. Richard Henderson along the Wilderness Trail to settle at Boonesborough and other Bluegrass points, but as many settlers came up the Kentucky River from the Ohio River as came down it. A flatboat ride downstream from Pittsburgh to the Kentucky River was easier, and less risky, than trekking across the uncertain, Indian-filled mountain trails. The mouth of the Kentucky was reached upstream of the treacherous Falls of the Ohio, at present-day Louisville, and settlers could pole up the River in flatboats during high water or travel in canoes during low water. Many took this route to their new Kentucky homes.

The second reason for the importance of the river to Kentucky is the abundance of natural resources within its headwaters region that had downstream markets, mainly coal and timber. Until the advent of railroads in the late 1800's, the Kentucky River was the only highway out of the mountains capable of carrying this bulky cargo. A major system of dams, that has few if any parallels in North America, was built to accommodate this traffic and remains today as one of the keys to the economy of central Kentucky, although not as a commercial highway as originally visioned. The commercial life of early Kentucky was totally dependent upon the Kentucky River, and many Kentuckians today who have never seen a barge or towboat still believe that commercial life can be restored to the waterway. It cannot, for many reasons, but a vivid memory of this commercial highway has been passed on to successive generations.

A third reason for this grip of the river upon Kentuckians is its natural beauty. It twists and turns upon itself along its entire route and is flanked at its midsection by the Palisades. The Palisades are sheer cliffs that rise from the banks of the river to a height of several hundred feet on both sides. Countless Kentuckians have spent their leisure hours cruising the river through this natural beauty just for the pleasure of boating and "getting away from it all." While cruising slowly through the Palisades, one can still sense the same feeling that Daniel Boone must have felt when he first paddled down the "Kaintuck" in 1769. Because of the rugged nature of these cliffs, little development has taken place in the Palisades, and other places as well, and the feeling of being far, far from civilization and the cares of the world is very real. The grip of natural beauty is very strong upon those who have enjoyed it and is not readily forgotten.

The bluegrass region is the spiritual home of Kentuckians. The rolling hills of horse farms wrapped in white fences with a stately mansion that can be glimpsed at the end of a long tree-lined driveway is the heaven to which many Kentuckians feel will be their ultimate reward. Being next to the basketball capital of the world is just that much more icing. The history of the bluegrass and the Kentucky River are intertwined as few rivers and a geographical area are. The Kentucky River only passes through the bluegrass area, but the feeling that it begins and ends there is vivid to many people.

The Kentucky River has been and still is many things to many people - a moving target. Even its name has changed. The name "Kentucky" is from the Iroquois word kentucke meaning prairie or meadow land. On the 1684 map by Franquelin the Kentucky River appears as the "Skipaki-cipi eu la Riviere Bleue" for an old Shawnee town in Clark County. On Charlevoix's 1744 map it is referred to as the Chonanono, while the 1756 map by Palairet is referred to as Milley's River. Early explorers such as Dr. Thomas Walker (1750) used Milley's River and Cuttaway River. Depending upon the tribe, other Indian names were Cuttawaba, Chenoka, and Chenoa, but Kentucke stuck and was used by the first settlers when they came to stay.

As the mighty Mississippi "... just keeps on rolling along." the Kentucky just keeps being reborn. This is the story of its five lives.

At the turn of the century, when Victorian manners were at their height, every proper home had a piano in the parlor and every proper young lady could play one. The family evenings often centered around this instrument without regard to talent. The sheet music that filled the piano bench was a bit mushy by modern standards, but well reflected the customs and mores of the day, especially those involving love, courtship, marriage, and despair. One of the few surviving songs that specifically spoke of Kentucky River life is typical of the thousands of songs that rolled from the presses of that day:

Where the Wandering Old Kentucky River Flows

Sparkling springs are rolling onward, Down the mountain far away,
Winding through the woodland pastures, Where sweet flowers bloom in May,
Near the shore of that clear river, Stands a cottage he well knows,
A voice within is sweetly singing, Where the wandering old Kentucky River flows.
  Chorus:
  The light is in her parlor, Dining room and hall,
  The steamboat is ringing, We hear the Captain call,
  Throw out the plank, bring down the grip and let the trav'ler out,
  The people are assembling there, We hear them laugh and shout,
  A maiden in the doorway stands, with arms extended wide.
  "Come back to me my roving lad, I'll be your loving bride,"
  The captain blows the whistle, Down stream he goes,
  Where the wandering old Kentucky River flows.

Years have flown since he last met her, In the land of love and light,
Weary now of boyhood roving, He must go back, if but tonight,
'Twas cruel fate that sent him strolling, To make a name he had to go,
They meet again with songs of greeting, Where the old Kentucky River flows.

Published by W. C. Piatt, Courier Boy, 1021 Wells Street, Chicago USA, Copyright 1916 by W. C. Piatt
Provided by Charles Parrish from Kentucky Historical Society files.

Life One

THE NATIVE YEARS

(Prehistoric to the late 1780's)

Long before Native Americans were called Indians by Europeans, the Kentucky River was the highway into the rich hunting grounds of central and eastern Kentucky, and before that it was a food source for a more primitive people.

The Native Years, or pre-history, of the Kentucky River basin are sketchy at best. Kentucky pre-history, its people and culture, is based upon the large number of stone weapons and tools that have been found in the excavated campsites, upon the burials that have been found and upon the few painted or scraped pictures that have been discovered on cave walls. From these relatively meager sources, some idea of the life, habits, diet, social structure, and degree of culture of the people of the various pre-history periods can be extrapolated.

For example, the excavation of a campsite yields the bones of the animals that were consumed by those occupying the campsite, as well as the remains of some of the seeds that were grown and eaten there. The examination of a burial often reveals the "treasures" of that person, particularly treasures that originated some distance from the site of the burial, hence an indication of trade with other groups. If several burials are found in an area, the social standing of each may be revealed by comparing the ornaments that are buried with each person. Stone points for weapons indicate how the weapon (spear or arrow) was used and what type of game the hunter was likely seeking. Stone tools, such as skin scrapers, tell us much about the daily life of the tool user and what he was able to do. The location of the campsites tells us whether the inhabitants were farmers and the size of the camp tells us about the social structure of the group. By assembling all the available facts and by the infusion of a vivid imagination, we can paint a reasonable picture of the life and times of early Kentuckians.

Archaeologists have divided eastern Kentucky pre-history into major periods based upon technology, social political structure, and general lifestyle*:[1]

End of North American Ice Age:	20,000 BC
Paleoindian:	9500 to 8000 BC
Archaic:	8000 to 1000 BC
Woodland:	1000 BC to 1000 AD
Fort Ancient:	1000 AD to 1700 AD
Historic:	1700 AD to Present

As the ice age came to an end with the recession of the ice cap northward from the Ohio valley, a migration across the Bering Strait into North America was taking place. We know relatively little about these people except they used crude stone weapons and tools. Their migration pattern took them around the headwater ends of the great rivers like the Mississippi, and they ultimately spread to most of the North American continent, including the Kentucky River basin.

We first meet the descendants of these ancient wanderers in the age archaeologists call the Paleoindian Period. Kentucky was colder and damper in those days as the ice age was relatively recent history and the rivers north of the Ohio River were in the process of being created as the waters from the melting icecap flowed southward. The rivers south of the Ohio, such as the Kentucky, were already in place,

*Different archaeologist assign slightly different dates to these periods.

but the climate was colder and the forests were filled with large animals, such as the mammoth, bison, mastodon, musk ox, stag-moose, and ground sloth. Evidence from the campfires of this period indicate that people functioned in small groups of about 20 persons (probably an extended family), had no social structure or ranking, and moved frequently from camp to camp. Overhanging rocks and caves were their homes, when they could find them.

These people had crude stone weapons and butchering tools, but no pottery for cooking. Bones of large animals have been found at their campsites in the Kentucky River basin, indicating that these animals were the makings of their meals. Bones of smaller animals such as deer, turkey, and rabbit, are not found at the campsites. It is likely that the larger animals were hunted because they were easier to hit with the crude, hand-thrown spears than the more fleet deer, turkey, or rabbit. The advent of the bow and arrow was still thousands of years in the future.

The probable hunting technique was to ambush the animals at the migratory river crossing points or at salt licks, both of which are common in the Kentucky River basin. The hunters, probably the men, would wait until the target had its head down to drink water or lick salt then stun or wound it with a spear. The other animals would flee, and the entire hunting party would descend upon the stunned animal for the kill. The meat from a mammoth could supply the group adequate food for several days as well as providing a good hide.

Fish and mussels from the river, as well as forest ready-to-eat food such as nuts, were a secondary part of the Paleoindian diet. Fish were probably caught by guiding them into a shallow part of the river and catching them by hand.

Several sites from the Paleoindian period have been found in the Kentucky River basin. All of them are located near a tributary to the river, with more in the headwaters area where the large game was attracted by the salt licks and mountain cover than in the blue-grass or lower river areas. It is likely that only a very small portion of the actual sites will ever be found.

As the icecap receded from Kentucky in terms of both years and miles, the climate became warmer and the megafaunta (mammoth, mastodon, etc.) game gave way to smaller animals such as the white tail deer. The extinction of the megafaunta may have been due to the change of climate, overhunting, or other unknown reasons, but the remains in the campfires of the next period, the Archaic Period (8000 to 1000 BC), show that the large animals had vanished from the diet of the people. The climate and the Kentucky River flow during this period reached about the status it is today, with the river still being the supermarket of the day, that is, where much of the hunting was done, mussels were collected, and fish were trapped.

Travel on the river was still hundreds of years away, but the design of stone weapons and tools within the basin indicates that groups living within the Kentucky River basin and on to the main Ohio River basin had contact with each other and traded ideas and goods. It is likely that all transportation was by foot, with the rivers serving as the guide to and from distant points. Burials indicate that a social structure was beginning to emerge as some burials were more elaborate than others.

The Archaic Period merged slowly into the Woodland Period (1000 BC to 1000 AD). By archaeological standards, this period is short, but several major changes were taking place that place this period in a category by itself: pottery was beginning to be used extensively; plants were beginning to be cultivated for food and fiber; a genuine social structure was emerging; and there was extensive trade and social contact between groups within the river system. The settlements (we could almost call them villages by now) in the Kentucky River basin were on the rolling ridgetops of the Bluegrass since the river flood plain was too confining and flood-prone for permanent settlements. The rockshelters in the upper Kentucky River basin offered seasonal campsites for hunting, but the remains of the campsites indicate that they were used only for short periods of time, probably weeks or a few months.

During this period burial mounds were being built along the Ohio River and many of its tributaries, such as the Kentucky River. These mounds indicate extensive contact between the peoples connected by the Ohio River system. Boat or canoe travel may have been known in this period based on the similarity of the mounds of the various groups within the Ohio River valley and partway up the Kentucky River, but such a connection is not certain. Footpaths along the river banks or shortcuts across the ridges may have been the mode of travel.

The moment at which man-made boats or dugout canoes first appeared on Kentucky River waters is not known, but they did appear at some time in the next period, the Fort Ancient Period (1000 AD to 1700 AD). It is possible that they were first developed elsewhere and the technology transferred to the Kentucky River groups. Long before this period, no doubt, some showoff pre-history lad had straddled a floating tree headed downstream to impress some pre-history lass, but the tree likely had both roots and limbs fully attached and was difficult to steer. Sometime during the Fort Ancient Period enterprising men observed that if the limbs and roots of a tree could be removed and the trunk cut into a manageable size, it could be guided downstream by a man straddling the log, and if the current were not too strong, the log could be pushed upstream by paddling with the hands. Removing the roots and limbs was not to be taken lightly as only stone tools and fire were available for the task. Trees most resistant to rot and disease were the most likely candidates for long-term use in the water.

It was probably soon observed that trees with sharp ends moved more easily through the water than those with blunt ones and that paddling with a stick was easier on the back than paddling with the hands. As the men became more proficient in felling and shaping trees, the concept of hollowing out the middle of large logs into a space in which the occupant could sit and carry cargo emerged, and the dugout canoe, which was in use at the time of the early explorers, was born. The task of hollowing out the middle of the logs was done with fire and a stone adz. Gum and rosin were spread on the parts to be burned out while the parts to be retained were kept wet. The charred wood was gouged out with the adz. The use of a dugout canoe to carry men and goods up and down the Kentucky River compared to walking the same distance would have about the same relationship as auto travel to airplane travel today. When the water was up, a dugout canoe could go from the three-forks area (Beattyville) to the Ohio River in about three days and back up in about seven days. By foot this trip would take several weeks. To their sorrow, the early settlers in the Bluegrass area would soon learn of the ease by which the Indians could ascend the Kentucky River to attack their riverbank settlements.

A DUGOUT CANOE

Native Americans in the Ohio River Valley developed a very efficient and durable dugout canoe made from a solid log. The only tools available to them were stone tools (an adz in this case) and fire. This picture shows them loading a dugout canoe.

Kentucky Archaeological Survey

The major mystery of the Fort Ancient Period was the abandonment of most of Kentucky by the people who had made it their home for several millennia. The remains of substantial permanent villages up to about 1400 AD have been found in many parts of the Kentucky River basin and other areas of Kentucky, but at the time the settlers crossed the mountains, there were no permanent villages in Kentucky. Several reasons have been advanced for this abandonment, including the intrusion of the Europeans with their diseases against which the Native Americans had no immunity, but historians and archaeologists have not settled on a single reason.

The remains of substantial permanent villages that existed before 1400 AD have been found in the Kentucky River basin and other areas of Kentucky. These remains indicate village populations of up to 300 with a developed social structure, pottery with decorations, cloth, and ritual trappings. There is extensive evidence of trade with groups several hundred miles away based on beads, metal objects, and stone types not native to the Kentucky River basin. Such trade would not have been possible without the speed and carrying capacity of the dugout canoe.

Whether these early Kentuckians died out or migrated to other places downstream is not known, but it is known that established tribes in Ohio, Indiana, and Illinois made frequent visits into eastern Kentucky in their canoes to seek the abundant game along the shores of the Kentucky River and to take the yields of their hunts back with them. To the tribes and people who frequented the Kentucky River headwaters area for game, the river was indispensable. Moving a heavy load of game out of the rugged mountains on their backs would have been virtually impossible. Loading it in dugout canoes and paddling downstream was easy. Based on the very large quantity of "Indian Rocks" (arrowheads) found in the Kentucky River headwater area, this process occurred with great frequency, especially considering the lack of major permanent settlements in the basin during this time. Their homelands were downstream in Ohio, Indiana, and Illinois, and many were on the banks of other tributaries to the Ohio River, making a single unloading of their cargo all that was necessary for most of them.

When Daniel Boone and other early explorers began their thrusts across the Appalachian Mountains, they had frequent encounters with the Indians, most of whom were on hunting trips from other areas. Fort Boonesborough was attacked by Indians arriving in canoes in 1778, and Stephen Frank, for whom Frankfort (Frank's Ford) is named, was attacked and killed by Indians who arrived by water. There are countless stories of the encounters of the early settlers and the peoples upon whose land they were settling, and many of these tales involve travel by river. The Europeans brought with them a higher technology of canoe-making, which included skins over willow frames, which were lighter and more maneuverable than dugouts, but were not as rugged.

Canoe travel on the Kentucky River during the summer and early fall was difficult at best and at times impossible. Today we look at the River below the three-forks area as though this is its natural state, but before the lock/dam system, it could be a series of pools and trickles interlaced with fallen trees and rocks during the dry season. During the flood season it could be a raging torrent and travel at that time was not possible for anyone. Viewing the Kentucky River with a macro eye, however, we realize it was a transportation corridor for Native Kentuckians that had no parallel.

Life Two

FLATBOATS AND KEELBOATS
TO THE DAWN OF STEAM.
(Late 1780's until 1842)

Early Explorers

The very early explorers of the Ohio River basin (before 1750) called the Kentucky River by whatever name they chose for their crude maps. To them it was just one more tributary of the Ohio River. Some of them may have ascended the river for a few miles, but little note was made of their efforts. There is also extensive evidence that trappers and other hunters from the eastern seaboard visited Kentucky before 1750 and probably built crude cabins, but they left little record of their sojourn in Kentucky, and we know little except that someone was here.

In the middle of the 18th century, the "colonies" were still under the firm thumb of the Georges of England. The good land east of the Allegheny Mountains was beginning to fill up, or at least that is the way they saw it, and entrepreneurs were eyeing the vast lands west of the mountains. In 1747 twenty prominent gentlemen of Virginia and Great Britain formed a company and petitioned King George II for a land grant west of the Allegheny Mountains. In 1750 they retained Christopher Gist to explore and report to them on the land for which they were petitioning King George. Gist approached the Kentucky River basin from the northwest and was the first to document his findings to the outside world. Little came of this report and the company for whom he worked, but it did, in a sense, put Kentucky on record.

Dr. Thomas Walker, physician and explorer, representing another group of land speculators, entered Kentucky likewise in 1750 from the Cumberland Gap, which he named. He and his party built a crude cabin as a base camp near present-day Barbourville in the Cumberland basin, but he traveled widely and reported on much of the Kentucky River basin. The initials "TW" were found carved on both sides of a large sycamore tree at the mouth of Station Camp Creek and have been attributed to him. He was also one of the first to report on the Indian practice of extensive land burning for the purpose of soil revitalization, which apparently had been in common practice for hundreds of years. Dr. Walker's report received a wide circulation and was the basis for the wave of colonists to soon follow.

The name "Daniel Boone" is the one most commonly associated with Kentucky exploration. He made many and extensive trips into Kentucky and on most of them he could just as easily have been killed as not. His first trip into Kentucky was in 1767, and he departed Kentucky for the last time in 1799 for Missouri when he was nearly 65 years old. He left his mark upon Kentucky in general and the Kentucky River basin in particular. He was arguably the best frontiersman the young country produced, but he was a bad businessman: he had claims to and lost all of vast tracts of land in every place he settled, including those in the Kentucky River basin. He died peacefully at 86 in Missouri, but his bones have been unpeacefully moved around and debated over ever since.

While Kentucky was still just three counties of Virginia (Fayette, Jefferson, and Lincoln), John Filson prepared the first map that actually resembles the geography of central Kentucky. His 1784 map of "Kentucke" was made from his own survey work as well as information supplied by Daniel Boone, James Harrod and oth-

Kentucky Historical Society, Courtesy of The Anschutz Collection

DANIEL BOONE

Daniel Boone's First View of Kentucky was painted in 1849 by William Tylee Ranney, a noted frontier and genre painter. It depicts the scene on June 7, 1769, when Boone and his hunting party – John Finley, John Stewart, Joseph Holden, James Monay, and William Cool – viewed the "beautiful level of Kentucke". Boone is authentically shown in a dark hunting shirt, leggings, moccasins, and the beaver hat indicative of his Quaker heritage. Set apart from the other members of the group, most of whom are in buckskin, Boone wears a red shirt and a red neckerchief, and also has a pack, powder horn, and hunting knife. He is pointing out features of the land to the rest of the party, most notably to a younger member of the group, the central figure of the painting. It is the passing on of frontier knowledge from the celebrated frontiersman and explorer to the next generation, who will populate the new land of Kentucky.

ers. It is centered on the Kentucky River basin and places the relationship of Dick's (Dix) River, the Red River, and the three forks (North, Middle, and South) in good perspective to the main stem of the Kentucky River and the adjacent basins (Cumberland, Licking, Green, and Salt). Frankfort is still called "Lee's-town," and Lexington is shown as the meeting point of many of the major roads of the day. This map was very widely used by new settlers and ultimately was published for French and German-speaking readers. His accompanying book, *The Discovery, Settlement, and Present*

State of Kentucke, was the standard guidebook for early settlers to Kentucky. Filson and his partners ultimately acquired about 800 acres of land at present day Cincinnati and helped found the city's early development. He disappeared in 1788 while surveying in Ohio, thought to have been killed by Indians.

Boonesborough

(Numerous historical artists have made the 1775 expedition of Daniel Boone into Kentucky at the head of would-be settlers to Boonesborough on behalf of Judge Richard Henderson and the Translyvania Company the most widely known early settlement west of the Allegheny Mountains.) A sturdy fort was built at Boonesborough, and an assembly of questionable legality was held there in 1775, a few hundred feet from the waters of the Kentucky River, for the express purpose of establishing representative government in the wilderness and to impart to the settlers some knowledge of the rights of the proprietors of the land, namely Judge Henderson and the Translyvania Company.

Kentucky was still part of Virginia in 1775, but the long arm of Virginia law did not reach to Kentucky, at least not in a meaningful way, at that time. Judge Henderson went through the motions of "purchasing" a 20 million acre tract of land between the Kentucky River and the Cumberland River from the Cherokees for 10,000 British pounds (or the equivalent thereof). This deal is known in history as the Treaty of Sycamore Shoals. The Cherokees, of course, had no concept of "owning" land, of 20 million acres, of 10,000 British pounds (or its equivalent), but after some discussion among themselves they agreed to take what Judge Henderson offered and stay out of the way for a while. The negotiations were adequate to clear Judge Henderson's conscience and he began to move settlers to the site that Daniel Boone selected on the shore of the Kentucky River which he called "Boonesborough." The deal with the Cherokees had no effect whatever on the Shawnees, who soon attacked the settlement.

Judge Henderson intended to run Boonesborough to his liking, but reality soon struck and little went right for him. The settlers who endured the hardships of the trek over the mountains did not intend to risk their lives to make Richard Henderson a rich man, and their first and last thoughts were of their own welfare. They simply did not do what Henderson asked them to do with regard to an organized community; each went his or her own way. The colony had some semblance of a real town, but was not a moneymaker for its founder. In 1776 the Virginia legislature began the necessary actions to nullify the "purchase" and Judge Henderson's ownership of this large tract of land. By 1778 the "purchase" was officially made null and void. Judge Richard Henderson soon faded from the pages of Boonesborough history.

The Boonesborough colony did, however, prosper to a small degree. It granted a franchise to operate a ferry across the Kentucky River in 1779 and shipped downstream what spare goods it had. It failed at its efforts to become the county seat and the state capital, but it did develop into a major center for tobacco shipment to New Orleans. Boonesborough appeared in the 1810 census as a separate town, but by the 1820 census its inhabitants were simply included into the county total population.

Early Navigation

Hard on the heels of Daniel Boone, who came down the river through the Cumberland Gap, and Captain James Harrod, who came up the Kentucky River via the Ohio River from Pennsylvania, settlers from the eastern seaboard began to stream across the Appalachian Mountains and up the Kentucky River. Their first thoughts were of their survival and defense from the Indians upon whose hunting land they were settling. For their farms the early settlers preferred the extensive plains of the uplands on both sides of the river to the limited bottom lands. The reasons for this choice were prudent: the bottom lands flooded extensively each year with flood levels exceeding 35 feet; the bottom lands were difficult to defend from the Indians, who used the precipitous cliffs as hiding places and points from which attacks were made; and the uplands were quite fertile. Only three towns were established directly on the River below the three-forks: Frankfort, Irvine and Beattyville. To this day each of these towns is subject to massive flooding, notwithstanding the efforts made by the Corps of Engineers for flood control. Above the three-forks (Beattyville), all of the towns are on a tributary of the Kentucky River: Jackson, Hazard, Whitesburg, Hyden, Hindman, and many others. These towns are subject to frequent flooding, but in the mountains there is no place other than the river bottom land on which to dwell.

By the late 1780's some degree of law, civilization and culture was taking hold in many places within the Kentucky River basin and thoughts could turn to more than just survival; they were thinking of making money. Agricultural products such as corn, pork, tobacco, dairy products, and rope-making hemp were in good supply, but hard currency was not. Ambitious men thought long and hard about means of converting the abundant agricultural products into cash, but there were major obstacles between Kentucky and ready cash: there were no roads to anywhere; the Appalachian Mountains separated Kentucky from the eastern markets; north and south of Kentucky hard money was also in short supply; and the likely down-river markets of Natchez and New Orleans, where there *was* money, were closed to Kentuckians by their Spanish rulers.

The Kentucky River was, nonetheless, the only pathway that could carry large amounts of goods to the outside world. The river, however, was not entirely user friendly. From mouth to headwaters, it was blocked with islands and shoals of rocky reefs, with overhanging trees and snags, with bars of gravel and drifting sand, and with sometimes very low water and sometimes very high water. To these natural obstacles were soon added man-made ones: timber booms, mills and fish dams. During the summer and fall months, stretches of the river were often a few inches deep, while in the winter and spring it could become a raging torrent with flood levels exceeding thirty-five feet. Natural obstacles are always re-occurring, and constant labor is required to keep them clear. Clearing man-made obstacles is far more difficult than clearing those caused by nature as clearing man-made obstacles involved the time honored application of political pressure. It was understood by those who wanted to use the river for the movement of goods and people that a slackwater or canal system would overcome the low-water and most of the other problems, but to Kentuckians of the late 1700's such a system was no more than fantasy.

When Kentucky became a state in 1792, it began to exercise some authority over its streams. Dams furnishing power for grist mills or other works benefiting the general public were allowed, provided they were built with locks and slopes. In the absence of bridges, dams were required to be at least 12 feet wide on crest with bridges over their pier heads and flood gates. Counties were given authority to declare streams navigable and the right to erect dams. Shortly before separation from Virginia, many streams were used for navigation, and the orders of the courts to construct mill dams were often contested. Petitioners appeared before the legislature praying for reversals of the orders for the construction of obstacles to navigation.

County fiscal courts were empowered to levy taxes and employ labor to maintain the channels for navigation, and some special problem areas were placed in the hands of commissioners appointed for that work. A bill introduced into the House on December 7, 1792, contained a resolution that the obstructions in the Kentucky River ought to be removed by the male-laboring "tithables" living within five miles of the river under the direction of an overseer appointed for that purpose. This labor would exempt them from similar work on the roads, a common practice at that time. Fines were established for those who failed to show up for their appointed tasks, with half of the fines so collected to go to the general stream improvement and half to the overseer. No records are available regarding the extent to which male laborers paid this tithe, but it is unlikely that they took the payment of political tithes any more seriously than their payment of ecclesiastical tithes. Most of the snags, etc. remained in place, and major commerce was not yet possible on the Kentucky River.

At this point the river was as much of an obstacle as it was a means of transportation. It separated settlement from settlement and during high water was not crossable. Far-seeing men, however, saw it as an unrealized opportunity.

General James Wilkinson

Kentucky has been amply blessed with its share of colorful men who sought their fortunes by skirting the law. The name of General James Wilkinson is near the top of this list. Had he devoted his immense talents, energy, and wit to the cause of freedom, his name could well be ranked with that of Washington, Adams, and Jefferson. He chose, instead, to deal in the undertow; always with a hidden agenda, but with the ability and wit to wiggle from beneath the debris with which he constantly covered himself. His name is associated with Aaron Burr and Benedict Arnold, with whom he had dealings during and after the Revolutionary War as well as numerous other men who have less than pristine records in American history. He was brilliant, resourceful possessor of a charismatic personality, had boundless energy, was utterly ruthless, and totally self-serving.

James Wilkinson was born of middle gentry in tidewater Maryland, where he rubbed shoulders with the local aristocracy, received a good education, and entered the Revolutionary War with no rank in the Maryland militia. He quickly caught the eye of General Horatio Gates and attained the rank of Brigadier General before reaching his 21st birthday. During the Revolutionary War he was involved in the "Conway cabal," which criticized Washington's weakness as a commander-in-chief and suggested that General Gates replace him. Wilkinson emerged from this debacle as a brigadier general and secretary of the Board of War of the continental Army when he was only twenty years old. Until the war's end he was constantly involved in controversy of various sorts, but always escaped intact. When peace came, he and his recent bride, of the prominent Philadelphia Biddle family, moved to Kentucky, where he had brothers-in-law in influential places. His war record, intellect, and magnetic personality quickly established him as a leader on the crude Kentucky frontier. He soon became involved in land speculation, salt mining, milling, shopkeeping, medicine (in which he had some training), and politics. His keen eye also saw a pair of aces that he intended to turn into a winning hand - a large quantity of agricultural goods in Kentucky and an untapped market for these goods in New Orleans.

Spain owned both sides of the lower Mississippi in 1783 and extracted from American traders a fee ranging from 25% of cargo value to outright seizure. At times the New Orleans and Natchez ports were totally closed, and at times they were partially open. Shipping goods to the lower Mississippi was risky business.

The difficulties notwithstanding, General James Wilkinson made his way in 1787 to New Orleans, running a gauntlet of snags, wild currents, Indians, bandits and bureaucrats with a flotilla of flatboats laden with Kentucky products, such as tobacco, hams, and butter to stand before Don Esteban Miro, Governor of New

Orleans and points beyond. The intent of General Wilkinson's endeavor was to open New Orleans to Kentucky products, with himself as the "monopoly" holder. Applying ample quantities of his charm and not too subtle hints upon his new Latin host, General Wilkinson explained to Don Esteban that it would be to his advantage to open his ports to Kentucky goods to prevent certain unruly Kentuckians from descending upon him. The Don, having no idea that Kentucky was 1000 miles away and wanting to avoid all disruption to his pleasant life, readily agreed to the idea, purchased the goods at hand on generous terms and entered into a private agreement with Wilkinson for other shipments of Kentucky goods to the ports under his control.

The original copy of the agreement has been lost, but Wilkinson preserved a second copy dated August 8, 1788, which granted him the right to ship $35,000 worth of Kentucky produce to Spanish territory and to import sugar and other commodities for shipment upstream. The document ordered all officers belonging to the Spanish government not only to refrain from any hindrance to the movement of his goods but also to render him every assistance that might be necessary—heady wording for one who had dreams of locking up the Kentucky-New Orleans trade.

The agreement was private for two reasons: there was an ongoing dispute between Spain and the newly independent United States that legally shut down all trade between the two countries; and specific sanction from Spain was required for a grant of commercial privileges to a foreigner. James Wilkinson, never one to let minor legal inconveniences stand in his way, proceeded as though they did not exist. The seats of both the Spanish and United States governments were far away, and much could be done before they heard of the venture or were in a position to do anything about it.

To get around the first inconvenience, Wilkinson rightly assumed that trade matters would soon be resolved between Spain and the United States. To get around the second inconvenience, Wilkinson apparently convinced Don Esteban that he intended to settle in New Orleans and become a law- abiding citizen of Louisiana; hence, he would no longer be a foreigner and could legally "import" goods from Kentucky.

Both the Spanish government of Louisiana and Wilkinson viewed two-way trade between New Orleans and Kentucky as highly desirable and profitable. To this end Wilkinson loaded a boat with $8,000 worth of merchandise bound upstream for Kentucky. A large part of the merchandise was lost in route due to the *"dilatory conduct"* of the crew and ice on the Ohio River. Because the Spanish government was interested in a long-term trade relationship with Kentucky, they reimbursed Wilkinson $6,121 for his loss. Apparently some of the merchandise did indeed reach Kentucky, for Don Esteban wrote Wilkinson a letter directing him on marketing techniques in Kentucky in order that trade would be built up between them. The letter directs Wilkinson not to sell his goods for more than they cost him in New Orleans because it was highly important that this *"first essay"* should inspire the inhabitants of Kentucky to further the trade. The letter reads, in part:[1]

> *I have good reason to expect that the arrival of the boats will produce the most agreeable sensation among those people and make them feel more keenly that their felicity depends on the concessions of such commercial facilities by his majesty and for the acquisition of which I conceive there are but few sacrifices which they would not make.*

We have no record of the prices that Wilkinson charged the Bluegrass nobility for these goods, but we do know that he was not inclined to sell anything at "cost."

General Wilkinson returned in grand style to Kentucky by sea via Charleston and Philadelphia. The gossip surrounding his return was that he had done more than sell tobacco in New Orleans. This suspicion was largely based on his sudden change in lifestyle, which was now very grand. He returned in state with a carriage, fine horses, servants, and the finest clothes Philadelphia could offer. The hospitality at his table was extravagant, all paid for with Spanish pieces-of-eight. Many of the farmers from whom his tobacco shipment was obtained failed to be paid. Heavy expenses of the trip, he claimed. Some of these farmers even provided tobacco for later voyages to New Orleans. A market for Kentucky produce was now open. Many hearts were happy, but some doubts lingered.

Soon after his arrival back at home in Frankfort, he began to assemble the produce, which he had gained the right to ship to New Orleans. Shipment was to be made from Louisville, but most of the produce would generate in the Bluegrass area, shipped down the Kentucky River to Louisville, thence down the Ohio and Mississippi Rivers. The ad placed in the December 5, 1787 *Kentucky Gazette* read in part:[2]

> *The subscribers are authorized by General Wilkinson, to purchase tobacco, tallow, butter, well cured bacon, hams, lard, and smoked briskets of beef, to be delivered on the Kentucke at the mouth of Hickman, the mouth of Dicks River, and General Scott's on or before the (20) twentieth of January next. The butter and lard to be in kegs not to exceed forty-five pounds net. These articles being intended for a foreign market it is necessary that they be handled in the manner not only to do the seller credit but to recommend our commodities to foreign merchants and make them desirous of engaging in a commercial intercourse with the western country.*[1]

The advertisement went on to list individuals who would inspect tobacco at the various receiving points on the Kentucky River.

It is also interesting to note that the shipment was to be made in the winter when the Kentucky River and the Falls of the Ohio could be negotiated and butter would not spoil en route to New Orleans.

The fleet assembled by Wilkinson consisted of 25 barges, some of which were mounted with three pounders, and were manned by 150 men who were additionally armed and prepared to fight if necessary. Indians as well as bandits were in good supply en route to New Orleans.

The Louisiana governor's son-in-law accompanied the small fleet, and it was said by some that the venture was as much political as it was commercial. The government of Louisiana (Spain) was encouraging settlers into their territory and had hopes of pulling some of the trans-mountain territory into their orbit and away from the newly formed United States. This encouragement was done by generous relaxation of duties on goods brought into Louisiana and the offer of cheap or free land. Many barges of goods were thus shipped from Kentucky to New Orleans by men who told authorities they intended to stay, bringing their families later, but had little real intention of doing any such thing. They just wanted to get their goods into the city duty-free then go back to Kentucky.

Wilkinson's private agreement with Don Esteban did not give him the monopoly he sought, but it did give him protection for his goods through Spanish territory. Legal trading with Spain was still not settled, but neither Wilkinson nor Bluegrass farmers gave much thought to that minor technicality. They were much more concerned with the shipment of their goods through the snags and shallows of the Kentucky River and over the Falls of the Ohio near Louisville. Many letters from Wilkinson (and other shippers) to his agents in New Orleans survive, describing and apologizing for the delays in shipments due to river mishaps. These letters describe leaky barges, running aground on the Kentucky River, sandbars, rocks, fallen trees, snags, floods, ice, Indian attacks, and just about every

GENERAL JAMES WILKINSON

General James Wilkinson is one of the most colorful and controversial men in Kentucky history. He is credited with opening the southern Mississippi ports of New Orleans and Natchez to Kentucky River produce when these ports were closed to trade by the Spanish authorities who controlled them in the 1780's. He also established a system of inspection and warehouses for the international tobacco market and laid out the City of Frankfort. He was a general in Washington's Revolutionary War army while 20 years old, but was constantly engaged in schemes and plots not altogether to the best interest of the newly minted United States.

Wilkinson had no formal military training, but after leaving Kentucky, he ultimately became Commander-in-Chief of the small United States Army. At various times in his long career he had dealings with both Aaron Burr and Benedict Arnold. He had a great fondness for military uniforms and brass, as seen in this picture which was apparently painted while he was the Commander-in-Chief. Following numerous scrapes with courts martial, in none of which he was convicted, he ultimately went to Mexico, where he served as military advisor to the Mexican Emperor. He died in Mexico and was buried in an obscure church cemetery there.

misfortune of which the mind can conceive on a river. A substantial portion of the goods never made it to market, but the markup in New Orleans was worth it. The shipper took the risk; that is, the farmer was paid for his produce at the going rate in Kentucky, and the markup in New Orleans was good enough to make up for the goods lost in route.

Wilkinson's main center of operations was Lexington, where he set up a store and managed his substantial financial and political empire. The chief money maker was tobacco, which was, and is, the chief legal money crop of the Bluegrass. Tobacco and other produce were loaded on barges in the Bluegrass area and shipped directly to New Orleans. The opening of the tobacco market to New Orleans was the single biggest shot-in-the-arm to the economic base of the Bluegrass, Kentucky River basin in general, and the Kentucky River commerce specifically. The local market within the Bluegrass—that is where tobacco could be transported by land was quickly saturated, but a virtually unlimited market downstream generated income not only for the growing farmer but also for the transportation industry as well.

A system of warehouses was established in both the Kentucky River basin and on the Ohio where tobacco could be stored waiting downstream conditions to be right for shipment. Inspection points were set up at key points on the Kentucky River, where the tobacco was inspected to make sure that it met the established quality standards of that day. Kentucky officials wanted to make sure that Kentucky tobacco was always welcomed in international ports.

In 1789 and 1790, when General Wilkinson's shipping empire was at its height, getting goods into New Orleans was still not easy or cheap. The duty on United States goods was 20%, and another 6% was extracted if the goods were transshipped to the United States from New Orleans on United States' vessels.

Wilkinson still had to feign his desire to become a Spanish citizen to obtain the permit to "import" goods to New Orleans. Others had to do likewise. The following is an extract from a letter written by Charles Wilkins to Judge Harry Innes describing trips from Pittsburgh to New Orleans in 1789 and 1790 (punctuation as written):[3]

> *It was the usual practice upon their arrival at Natchez for owners and Boat crews to take the Oath of Allegiance to the King of Spain; It was practiced by those who went to that country at the time alluded to above to induce the Spanish officers to believe, that it was their intention to become subjects & as preparatory to this step & previous to obtaining a passport to proceed, the Oath of Allegiance was*

administered, upon which a passport was granted, or permission to sell at Natchez was procured. Americans who migrated to that Colony were permitted to sell their property free of duty.

Various modes were adopted to evade the payment of the duties by adventures to New Orleans, and it was practiced by others as well as myself, to petition the Governor for a grant of land under the pretense of becoming an inhabitant & I was induced to believe that the mildness of his Catholic Majesty's Colonial government was always spoken of with praise.

General James Wilkinson himself was a master at the subterfuge of pretended allegiance change. On March 17, 1791, Wilkinson wrote a long letter from Frankfort to his agent in Lexington, Mr. Hugh M'Ilvain, detailing instructions for evading Spanish navigation laws. This letter reads, in part:[4]

When you come within six leagues of Lance a la Grace get with a canoe and two hands, push down to the command and order the boats to go on without waiting,—you will show the invoice of your Cargo and the list of your hands to the Commandant, make him a small present, beg him to pardon your hurry and push the boats – never halt anywhere after this before you reach Natchez unless at night. When you get to that place put on your best Bib & tucker and wait upon the Governor or Commandant, with your invoice, manifest, and the list of your Crew with their several occupations. Deliver your letters and inform him that you have come down with as many of the hands as you can persuade into the humor to make Establishments in the

Province, and request him to administer the Oath of Allegiance, of which, when done take a certificate to show that you are a subject. Make him a present, beg his passport for New Orleans and proceed as speedily as possible – at the little ports along the river between that and New Orleans you must go or send ashore in a canoe and exhibit your passport to several Commandants—when you arrive in New Orleans be ready dres'd and wait immediately upon the Governor, with your letters, certificate of Allegiance, invoices, manifest & list of your crew—anybody will show you the way to the Governor, or perhaps a Sergeant may carry you to him as this is customary. Say to the Governor, that having formed a determination to make settlement in Louisiana you have invested some of your property in tobacco, which should be happy to furnish to the Royal Magazine, if it should be wanted, and that in the meantime you should thank his Excellency for permission to store in the Kings magazine—To his Inquiries respecting Kentucky, say nothing that is not flattering to Louisiana. Say that the ignorant and low class of people with very few reputable characters, such as Marshall Scott & Muter, are hostile to Spain but that the judicious Intelligent men of the Country, know the importance of supporting an amicable intercourse;—consider me the head of those Characters and pay me other complements you may think I deserve....Inform him that you are bred to commerce but that your principal view is settling in Louisiana, was to establish several useful and valuable manufactories in Comp'y with Gent'm who you expect after you in two or three weeks.

The original letter is several times as long as the above quote and it shows plainly that General Wilkinson well knew the realities of Spanish protocol. Mr. M'Ilvain would have done well to heed the General's advice.

General Wilkinson failed to become rich from the trade doors he had opened, but he always seemed to have ready cash. His Frankfort store was stocked, in part, with New Orleans goods and he was building a "mansion" in Frankfort. He made more shipments to New Orleans, but in smaller quantities. Some suppliers were still unpaid. From time to time pack mules with saddles of Spanish manufacture and heavy saddle-bags that clinked appeared for him in Frankfort. "Tobacco money," Wilkinson said. "Spanish pension money," said the local wags.

Wilkinson returned to the army in 1791 and ultimately became the Commander-in-Chief of the small armed forces of the new nation. His army life continued to be spotted with scandal, including a possible involvement with the nebulous Aaron Burr western enterprise, several courts martial from which he was never convicted, and more mule loads of Spanish pieces-of-eight (back payment for tobacco, he always said).

The army scandals and political pressures finally caught up with him, and he resigned from the army to become the military advisor to Emperor Agustin de Iturbide of Mexico[5]. He died peacefully in bed and was buried in an obscure church in Mexico. Wilkinson carried to his grave in 1825 many secrets that the living would like to have had answered. These well-kept secrets are a testimony to his ingenuity, skills, and ability to always land on his feet, even when dropped from high places. Several researchers in the late 19th and early 20th centuries discovered papers and documents in Spain and Cuba that establish a paper trail, a story that would excite most novelists.

His footprints upon the Kentucky River and the people within its basin, however, are still plain: he made tobacco a viable cash crop; he showed that the Kentucky River was a workable artery of commerce from the heartland of Kentucky to the international Port of New Orleans; he established a system of inspecting and grading tobacco for foreign markets; he established a system of tobacco warehouses whereon tobacco could be stored prior to the right river conditions for shipment; he opened markets for other Kentucky produce such as pork, beef and beef products, hemp (rope making); and he brought hard currency into Kentucky (four "mule loads" of money) where the principal medium of exchange had been barter with pelts and land warrants. Late in his life General Wilkinson wrote, in his own defense, true words: *These voyages to New Orleans cost me upwards of a thousand guineas and the community of which I was a member profited by my toils, perils, and expenses.*[6]

By far the most significant impact General Wilkinson had upon the Kentucky River was to show the need to improve the river into a more reliable commercial artery. During many months of the year a vessel no larger than a canoe could navigate the river and even then it would have to be portaged around sand bars, snags, and other obstacles. Even when the river was at a navigable stage, a large percentage of cargo originating in the Kentucky River basin never made it as far as the Ohio River. For the most part the farmers had been paid for the goods before shipment, but the price paid them had to be "discounted" to take into account the certain losses in transit. From both the farmer grass roots level as well as to the trading merchant level, pressure was put upon the local political structure to "do something about the Kentucky River."

Flatboats and Keelboats

Flatboats in abundance did, however, begin to make their way from the Bluegrass of Kentucky, down the Kentucky, Ohio, and Mississippi Rivers to the Spanish ports from which they had recently been banned. Their cargoes were the goods that the Bluegrass was well suited to provide: tobacco, hemp for rope making, smoked pork, beef, potatoes, apples and other agricultural products. One of the more famous Kentucky products began to appear on the markets at this time, Kentucky bourbon. A bushel of corn fetched about fifty cents and was not worth the boat trip down river, but a bushel of corn could be converted into three to five gallons of good whiskey worth one to two dollars per gallon on the open market, and there was always an open market for Ken-

FLATBOATS, KEELBOATS, AND SAILS

These are the pre-steam types of boats used on the Kentucky River to haul freight and passengers. The flatboat in the lower left was by far the most common freight and passenger hauler. It went downstream with the current as its power. The keelboat in the middle of the picture was used for upstream travel. It was pushed by men thrusting their poles into the river bottom then walking to the back of the boat while pushing it under their feet. They would then remove their poles, go to the front and begin the process again. The keelboat could haul far less cargo than a flatboat, but generally it carried more valuable goods upstream than the flatboat carried downstream. The sailboat shown in the rear was seldom used on the Kentucky River, but sometimes sails could be raised on the much wider Ohio and Mississippi Rivers.

tucky whiskey. Many converted bushels of Kentucky corn therefore made their way down the Kentucky River to slake the thirst
within countless Spanish throats in the lower Mississippi.

The flatboats, or barges, were the workhorse arks of the river.
They were square at both ends, from twenty to fifty feet long,
ten to fourteen feet in width, and drew about three feet of water
when fully loaded with 30 to 60 tons of cargo. The gunwales
were 6"x6" solid oak timbers, while other planking was no thinner than 1_" and much of it was 3" thick. The sidewall planking
relatively high, (about five feet), were originally intended more
to defend against Indian attacks than to defend against river
bandits. A part of the flatboat was generally partitioned off with
an arched roof for the use of paying passengers (the crew slept
in the open deck). Since many of the down stream voyages were
in the dead of winter, some degree of comfort was needed if they
expected paying passengers on board. The boats were propelled
by the river current, but one or more pairs of large oars were
placed on each side to guide the flatboat around snags, sandbars, and through the Falls of the Ohio. A large oar or "sweep"
was at the stern for guiding the vessel. The flatboats were built
to withstand the Falls of the Ohio at Louisville, collisions with
rocks, strong currents, and the several weeks in the water. Provisions were placed on board for the entire voyage as pulling into
shore for supplies was an invitation for river bandits. The downstream trip took from six weeks to three months, depending upon
river conditions and any mishaps that might occur.

In addition to the cargo on the flatboats, the flatboats themselves were cargo. The voyage to New Orleans was one-way for
the flatboats; there was no way to get them back up river. They
were, therefore, sold for timber or firewood at their destination.
Many fine homes in the lower Mississippi were framed from oak
timber that had served its initial duty in a Kentucky River flatboat.

When the crews reached their destination in New Orleans, they were disbanded and left to their own devices to make their way back to Kentucky. Many returned afoot through Mississippi and Tennessee with Spanish silver in pouches slung over their shoulders. In this portion of the journey, they faced far greater dangers on the Natchez Trace from robbers than they ever faced on the water. Most of the time they traveled in groups for as much security as a group could offer, but the robbers often had larger groups and the crews returned empty handed to their Kentucky homes. Some of the more enterprising crew members invested their wages in luxury goods in New Orleans that would command a very high price in Kentucky and returned to Kentucky via keelboat. Others went on by sea to markets on the Atlantic coast where they purchased merchandise, sent it over the Wilderness Road, or brought it to Pittsburgh or Wheeling by packhorse or wagon

Louisville District, U.S. Corps of Engineers

FLATBOAT – THE ARK OF THE FRONTIER

This rugged craft was built to carry about 30 to 60 tons of bulky cargo and a few brave passengers. They were built from heavy, handsawed lumber and could be put together by men of modest carpentering skills. The minimum plank thickness was about 3-inches, and the gunwales were much heavier. Plank seams were filled with tar to make them watertight. The sidewalls were semi-forts against Indian and later bandit attacks. Some carried a small cannon. The crew generally sat, ate, and slept on top of the enclosure. Paying passengers rode inside. Creature comforts were scarce for all, but frontier-bound families generally found traveling to their new homes by flatboat more comfortable than overland travel. Flatboats carrying cargo to the southern Mississippi ports of Natchez or New Orleans were generally sold for their lumber value or firewood.

and shipped down the Ohio to eager Kentucky shopkeepers. Commerce thereby moved in a complete water and land circle beginning and ending in the Kentucky River basin.

The upriver journey from New Orleans, when it was made, was totally different from the downstream trip; flatboats could float downstream but not upstream. Power was needed to do that, and a flatboat has no power. Keelboats, which carried a much smaller, but more valuable cargo of goods, were propelled by poles. Facing backward, a deckhand would walk to the front of the boat, thrust a long pole into the river bottom, and walk to the rear of the boat along the side of the deck, essentially pushing the boat along under his feet and against the pole as he walked. When he reached the rear of the boat, he extracted his pole from the river bottom and repeated the process. It took many a walk along deckside to go from New Orleans to Frankfort, but there was no other way. Small sails were used also, but they could not be counted upon for upriver winds at all times. A keelboat carried about 20 to 30 tons (about half that of a flatboat) and took about twice as long to make the same journey. The high markup of luxury goods in Kentucky, however, made up for this cost, time, and energy.

"Bushwhacking" was also used to some degree on the Kentucky River when moving against the current. With this technique a deckhand would grab an overhanging bush and walk to the rear of the boat pushing the boat under his feet as he walked while hanging on to the bush. Plainly this technique could be used only where there were bushes to pull on and was not for the fainthearted.

The Tobacco Warehouse and Inspector

Modern highways and federal government regulations have now taken the marketing of tobacco far from the banks of the Kentucky River, but the marketing of tobacco and the rise of the Kentucky River as an avenue of commerce actually grew up together.

The birth of both took place when James Wilkinson opened the New Orleans market to Kentucky tobacco in 1787. Prior to that date, tobacco was grown in Kentucky, but not on a large, commercial scale. Settlers with Virginia and North Carolina roots planted it when they came across the mountains, but it was grown and used by local smokers, was transported overland and by water a few miles, and varied widely in quality. Wilkinson changed all that.

From its very early days as an English colony, Virginia was a tobacco supplier to the mother country. English law stipulated that all tobacco grown in the colonies had to be shipped to England on English ships by English merchants. The Revolutionary War, of course, changed that, but since Kentucky was still part of Virginia until 1792, Virginia law still determined how tobacco was to be marketed on the local basis. Virginia law called for the state legislature to establish tobacco warehouses at key places and for the county courts to appoint inspectors to examine the tobacco. The inspectors would stamp the casks as to the grade of tobacco it contained and issue a note or warrant to the owner of the tobacco. These notes served as legal tender for many years on the currency-less frontier. Virginia law provided that forgers or counterfeiters of these notes were liable "*. . . to suffer death without benefit of clergy.*". The inspectors received a fee for the tobacco they inspected set a rate (by the legislature) that was to provide them with an adequate, but not lavish, living. They were bound to be on duty at the warehouse from October 1 through the following August 10 of each year with the exception of Sundays, Christmas, Easter and three days at Whitsuntide. This last holiday was a relic of the days when the Anglican Church was the state church of Virginia. It was observed on the seventh Sunday after Easter and the following Monday and Tuesday.

The Inspector was paid 6 shillings for each hogshead inspected. An additional 3 shillings and 6 pence were charged for prizing the tobacco and for the nails used in the construction of the wooden hogs-head. These wooden containers had staves no more than 48" long and were no more than 30" across at the head. They were required to hold at least 1000 pounds of tobacco. Each September the inspector had to report to the county court on the number of hogsheads received and shipped out of their respective warehouses. The court also paid out money to holders of receipts at this same time.

The tobacco warehouses themselves were authorized by the legislature to specific individuals who had a good reputation in the local community and would rent space to the inspectors for the performance of their duties and for the tobacco while it was awaiting shipment downstream. The very early warehouses, that is prior to 1803, were log structures, but likely had wooden floors for the storage of tobacco. After 1803 Kentucky law required them to be made of stone, brick, strong boards, or logs and to be completely weatherproof. The owner of the warehouse was to provide the scale, weights, and other tools necessary for the handling, inspection, and storage of the tobacco. The state was responsible for the tobacco in case of fire.

When Kentucky became a state in 1792, Virginia law was more or less adapted, until specifically changed. The designation of the location of the warehouses was still a state function, and the appointment of inspectors was still a county affair. There was a constant pull and tug as to where the warehouses would be, who would own them, and how far apart they could be and still maintain financial integrity. A permit to operate a tobacco warehouse assured a rather steady source of income. Local political influence was needed to operate a tobacco warehouse.

The impact that James Wilkinson had upon tobacco and tobacco inspection was to increase both the quantity and quality of tobacco grown in Kentucky. Prior to his opening up the New Orleans market, a relatively small quantity of tobacco was grown in Kentucky as there was a very limited market for it. The quality of the tobacco was up to the resolution of the individual grower and what he thought the local market would purchase. Wilkinson changed all that: he saw to it that more tobacco warehouses were opened, that the inspectors were men who would diligently do their job, that there was a standard grading system for tobacco, and that a good supply of tobacco would appear on the market. He knew that his reputation was at stake when a hogshead of tobacco was opened in New Orleans. It had to be what it claimed to be. Some of his tobacco was actually used in New Orleans, but most of it entered the international market and was directed to Spain. Some of his tobacco was downgraded in New Orleans, a point that caused him great consternation for several years.

Wilkinson generally took tobacco on consignment; that is, the farmer was not paid until the tobacco was sold in New Orleans and the money brought back to Kentucky. The farmer was to be assessed a fee for shipping his tobacco down the river, which would be paid for first out of the sales proceeds, then the farmers would be paid 15 shillings per hundredweight of his tobacco. If there were any money left over after that, it was to be divided two thirds to the shippers and one third to Wilkinson. Some farmers saw little of their money from this arrangement. Heavy expenses said Wilkinson.

The first tobacco warehouse actually built in Kentucky was below the Falls of the Ohio at present-day Shippingsport under the 1783 Act (Virginia). This Act also authorized warehouses at Leestown and the Mouth of Hickman, but these were probably not built until 1787 as there was no need for them. After Wilkinson opened the New Orleans market in 1787, Virginia authorized warehouses at the Mouth of Dicks (Dix) River, Harrods Landing, Mouth of Craigs Creek (General Scotts land), Boonesboro, on the land of John Collier in Madison County, Stone Lick Creek at Steeles Landing (near Tyrone), and the Mouth of Jacks Creek in Madison County.

The warehouse previously authorized in Leestown was built on Wilkinson's land in Frankfort. In addition to these warehouses being built on the land of prominent local citizens, the sites had to be accessible by land, near a ford in the river where tobacco could be carted across when the river was low, and have some flat land for the local enterprises that would spring up around the warehouse. All of these sites became small settlements or towns, but none have survived as towns (except Frankfort) because of flooding. The Kentucky River has a 35'-38' flood stage that extends far back on both shores and places any structures therein at constant risk. Frankfort continues to suffer from this risk and survives behind a floodwall built in recent years by the Corps of Engineers.

Wilkinson's personal involvement in the tobacco was relatively short-lived: from 1787 until his last shipment in 1791. Mule loads of Spanish pieces-of-eight continued to be delivered to him well after 1791, but he claimed this was for tobacco that had initially been downgraded then later sold at market prices. The real truth will never be known.

It is known, however, that James Wilkinson forever changed the face of Kentucky economy: he made Kentucky into an international factor in the tobacco market. The system of tobacco warehouses, inspectors, and grading that he started in 1787 survived far beyond his lifetime and brought countless millions into Kentucky pockets.

River Improvements, the Beginnings

Nothing could be done to control the course of the river or nature, but the snags could be removed. In 1792 the Kentucky legislature chartered a company to clear the channel of snags from Frankfort to the mouth and collect a toll for their efforts. The counties along the shores of the river were authorized and encouraged, for their own sake, to undertake river-clearing efforts, but little or nothing came of this effort, and the flatboats had to wind their way between snags and shoals until they reached the Ohio.

In July of 1799 the first semi-organized "report" of the river problems was heard by the legislature, but as this legislature was consumed with the writing of a new state constitution, the report fell upon deaf ears. The report was made by Martin Hawkins and contained a list of seventeen items needed to clear the river from Frankfort to the Ohio River. An example of the items on the list includes:[7]

REMARKS ON THE IMPROVEMENT OF
THE KENTUCKY RIVER

1. When the river is 14 inches deep at the island opposite to Frankfort; the fall to the lower end of the fish trap is 900 yards long and the whole descent is 60 inches. There appears to be a small bar entirely across the river here, which to make the channel complete would require some blowing of the rock: but the river might be made tolerably passable by an expense of 50 dollars in straightening the sluice and deepening it, so as that boats drawing 15 inches of water will pass when the river is lowest. $50

9.Cedar (Creek) 1,000 yards; 100 inches fall
This fall is occasioned by the stone thrown into the river from the creek; as are almost all the fall in the river. The stones are small and might easily be moved. To straighten this fall, which is the worst in the river, will take about 300 dollars: but it might be made tolerably passable, at an expense of about 150 dollars; and that sum at least, must be laid out here. $150

13. Clay Lick (Creek) 70 yards; 6 inches fall
Here is a Sycamore tree that reaches entirely across
the river, on which you may cross without wetting
your feet. In low water every boat that passes is
obliged to unload, and be dragged on dry land round
it. The losses sustained by adventurers, with labour,
that this tree has cost within five years has been esti-
mated at 3,000 dollars.   *$ 30*

The total "Expence" estimated by Mr. Hawkins was $920, which
he rounded up to $1,000 in a footnote to his report, a reasonable
sum to clear the channel from Frankfort to the Ohio even in those
days. He also noted that about $500 should be set up to clear trees
on either side of the river so that a reoccurrence of the Clay Lick
sycamore tree would be eliminated. There is no record of how much
Mr. Hawkins was paid to prepare the report.

On December 19, 1801, the Kentucky Legislature chartered "The
Kentucky River Company" to clear the river from its mouth on the
Ohio River to the mouth of the South Fork (near present-day
Beattyville). The capital stock of $10,000 was to be subscribed in
$50 shares by the counties contiguous to the river. Commissioners
would be appointed from each county to remove all barriers which
they judged would *impede or obstruct the passage of boa*ts, and of
other hindrances the removal of which would be obstructions of
the stream at the rate of $2 for each 24 hours of obstruction. The
right to collect tolls was granted to the company. The tolls were $4
for a 30' boat up to $6 for a 60' boat. Beyond a 60-foot boat, the toll
was $0.09 per foot.

The task of clearing the river seemed too great for even such a
substantial body of men, and nothing was really accomplished,
but the need for a cleared river to sustain the traffic both up and
down the river was increasing. The Legislature regrouped, and on

January 10, 1811, they approved a $10,000 lottery whereby the river was to be cleared similar to the 1801 Act except the clearing was to extend up Goose Creek, the chief tributary of the South Fork, to the salt works of James Garrard and Sons in Clay County. Commissioners were appointed, and time extensions granted, but nothing was done. Rural Kentuckians of 1811 had no vision of one of the great inventions of the 19th century that would remold energy and transportation for the next 150 years—the steamboat.

From 1813 to 1818 local stabs at improving the river for local commerce were made, particularly in the headwaters where salt was a major industry and the manufacturing of iron was beginning in the Red River area and near Station Camp Creek. This clearing work involved projects of local nature for specific industries along the river. The small amount of work done on the Kentucky River between 1813 and 1818 was the forerunner of 100 years of substantial improvement of the river. The vision of General Wilkinson of extensive commerce with the world was beginning to be realized, but no one knew it or gave him any credit for his vision or efforts.

Commerce

Prior to General Wilkinson's endeavors in trade with New Orleans, traffic on the Kentucky River was largely local "shifting" of goods between river settlements, but when tobacco became an item of international trade for Kentucky farmers, there were substantial changes to the way business was done on the Kentucky River. The primary trade item "shifted" early on the river was salt. Every settler and settlement had, of course, to have salt. Within the headwaters of the Kentucky River there were many salt licks and wells were dug into them that discharged salt water with a higher salt content than sea water. There was ample wood to burn to reduce the brine to marketable salt. Many of the early improvements sought for on the river were to access salt producing works. In the absence of hard currency, pelts or other items of barter were used to purchase salt.

General Wilkinson saw that salt was an important and relatively profitable commodity on the Kentucky frontier. Two letters by him to his agent, Mr. Massie, concerning salt have survived. They read, in part:[8]

Danville, December 10, 1786

> *Dear Sir: — I beg you to proceed with all possible dispatch to the falls. You will call by the lick and urge the provision of the salt; and prepare some way of conveying it to the river. You will make the rest of your way to Nashville and there dispose of it for cotton, beaver furs, raccoon skins, otter, etc. You must always observe to get as much cash as you can ....When you received the salt take care to have it measured in a proper honest way with a spade and shovel with no shifting, etc............*

A follow-up letter:

Fayette, 29th Dec. 1786

> *Dear Massie: — I approve of your plan to go to the port with two hundred bushels of salt and sell for cash or furs but take no deer skins. Be sure to get as many otters as possible. Be cautious in your movements, guard against savages coming and going and discharge your men the moment you get to the port. The only thing you have to dread is the ice. To be caught in the ice would be worse than the devils own luck. Act with decision and dispatch in whatever you do. God bless you.*

> *J. Wilkinson*

Commerce on the Kentucky River, as well as the other rivers pointing to New Orleans, experienced an upward surge in activity immediately before and after the turn of the 19th century for three reasons, all of which were beyond their control. All of Europe was consumed with keeping Napoleon at bay, which meant that European food-producing systems were in shambles and needed all the food that the New World could provide. This need was further stimulated by the fighting in the Caribbean among the colonies of the respective belligerent European nations. This was mainly naval warfare, but sailors do need to eat and this food could come best from the newly-emerged United States, which had far more land for growing crops than it had mouths to consume it.

The second reason for the spurt of commercial growth was the 1795 Treaty with Spain (actually signed on April 25, 1796), which was good for three years and guaranteed the United States the right to deposit goods in New Orleans and to export them without paying *any other duty than the fair price for the hire of the stores.* When the three-year period expired, no provision was made for its extension or for another place to deposit goods, and the trade stopped for the moment. These difficulties were soon settled by the third reason: the Louisiana Purchase of 1803. While the United States was bickering with Spain about the right to transfer goods at New Orleans, Spain was in the process of transferring all of Louisiana, extending from New Orleans to the Pacific northwest, to France. France, in turn, made the United States a good offer for this substantial tract of real estate. The United States now owned the Mississippi basin, and more. The wars in Europe were coming to an end, for the moment, and this market slowed down, but the Port of New Orleans was now available to ship Kentucky goods to the world.

With the Mississippi now available for the uninterrupted passage of United States ships, the time for regular shipping service was at hand, both up and down the Kentucky River as well as the other rivers in the Mississippi basin. A prelude (before the Louisana Purchase) to regular shipping service appeared in the *Cincinnati Centennial of the North-Western Territory* in 1795:[9]

> *Notice.— The subscriber informs the gentlemen, merchants and immigrants to Kentucky, that he will be at the mouth of the Kentucky river on the first day of February next with a sufficient number of boats to transport all goods, etc., which they may think proper to entrust him with up the river. He will also keep a store-house for the reception of any goods which may be left with him. Carriage of goods to Frankfort, 50 cents per hundred; to Sluke's warehouse, 75 cents; to Warwick 100 cents; Dicks River, 125 cents,*
>
> *Mouth of the Kentucky, Jan 15, 1795*   *Elijah Craig, Jr.*

Mr. Craig was looking for goods manufactured in the Cincinnati area to be floated to his place of business at the mouth of the Kentucky River (Carrollton) to be poled up-stream to the Kentucky River towns.

Another ad for shipment down the Kentucky River is found in the *Palladium* published in Frankfort:

THE BOATING BUSINESS

> *The subscriber having furnished himself with several good BOATS, and engaged a number of experienced HANDS, respectfully offers his Services to Merchants, Traders, and Others, who may have Goods, etc., to send to any place on the Western waters.*
>
> *Those who may think proper to employ him, may rest assured that the greatest care will be taken of the articles confided to him, and the strictest punctuality observed in the delivery.*
>
> *John S. Travis*
> *Port-William (Mouth of the Kentucky) September 3, 1798*
> *Warehouse-Room for depositing Goods can be had as above.*

This service was not regular, but it was the prelude to it. The moods of the Kentucky River were too undependable for regular service to float downstream or pole upstream on a calendar basis, but shippers could more or less plan ahead for shipments, and the threat of confiscation by a foreign power was now lifted. In the early days of merchandising, the large planters generally made the downstream trip with their goods, looked after them on the way down, bribed Spanish agents for passage if necessary, and bartered for their sale at their destination. A class of middlemen now arose who would either purchase the goods from the planter or serve as an honest agent for the planter. True regular service on the Kentucky River was just around the next bend—steamboats.

The papers of that time also contained numerous ads for boat hands. The "cruise" down and the walk back up to Kentucky took about five to six months, if all went well. The downstream portion of the voyage had to be in the winter, not only because that is when the water was high enough to float a boat, but also to keep the agricultural goods (butter, lard, flour, beef products, pork products) from spoiling. This, of course, was very taxing upon the health of the crews, aside from the Indian and bandit attacks going and coming. In 1817 the Kentucky Legislature established a hospital in Louisville near the Falls-of-the-Ohio, where the crews often had layovers due to low water on the falls. The preamble to the Act establishing the Hospital reads, in part;[10]

> *Whereas it is represented that of those engaged in navigating the Ohio and Mississippi rivers many persons, owing to the fatigue and exposure incident to long voyages become sick and languish at the town of Louisville where the commerce in which they are engaged sustains a pause occasioned by the falls of the Ohio River; that the charity of the citizens of that town and country is no longer able to administer to these poor unfortunate persons the support*

and attention which the necessities of the latter and the humanity of the former would seem to demand and pre-scribe; . . . .

The Mississippi legislature implored Congress that:

A citizen who performs a voyage of two or three thousand miles upon our inland waters and subjects himself to the horrors of shipwreck, poverty, and disease far from his home and his friends is surely as much entitled to the charitable provisions of Congress as the mariner who makes voyage upon the ocean.

This was likewise a plea from Mississippi for the Federal government (who at that time offered some health benefits to the maritime industry) to look after inland sailors in the same manner it looked after sea-going sailors. The care of sick flatboat hands returning home was a burden on Mississippi just as it was on Louisville.

The final port of debarkation from Kentucky was Louisville, where there was a government inspector. From that point, the journey to New Orleans would take 30 to 60 days, traveling day and night, rain or shine. All provisions for the voyage were on board. The crew generally consisted of one chief, who received about $100, and four hands, who received about $50 each. In New Orleans, Kentucky boat hands were well known, though not altogether favorably. They did what sailors from time immemorial have done after two months at sea on bad food and water. From New Orleans they had to make their way back to Kentucky by foot (1,000 miles) or by sea to Philadelphia, Pittsburgh, then down the Ohio to Kentucky. Most of the hands returned to Kentucky with little of the $50 in their pockets.

Although not directly on the river, Lexington emerged as the commercial center of Kentucky. The roads, such as they were, converged in Lexington, and it became the place where merchants and later manufacturers lived. In 1803, Lexington had over 3,000 in-habitants while Pittsburgh had but 2,000. Lexington became the banking center of the state, and in 1802 an inland marine insur-ance company was chartered specifically for river commerce. The insurance would pay when the losses exceeded five percent of the cargo value and would pay up to five-sixths of the total value of the lost goods. Inland marine insurance was a great help to the small shipper as virtually all of a small merchant's net worth could be tied up in a single voyage. Some hard currency and credit in major eastern cities became available to the shippers on the Ken-tucky River through the Lexington merchants.

During the very early years of the 19th century, the cargoes began to shift from raw agricultural products to processed agricultural goods and manufactured goods, mainly from Lexington. Flour, shipped in 95-pound barrels, followed by meat products and hemp were the chief products to enter the Port of New Orleans from Kentucky. Hemp, for rope making, had been grown in the Bluegrass by the very early set-tlers, first from necessity, then for export. The shipment of raw hemp as well as products made from hemp was a major export from the Bluegrass until about 1870 when these commodities were replaced by other materials, such as sisal, jute, and Manila hemp. Other manufac-tured articles from the Bluegrass included soap, paper, powder, and nails. Tobacco continued to be shipped out, but it began to lose in its percentage of exports. Bourbon, first made in Kentucky in 1789, was welcomed in any port.

Flatboat Life and Times

Myth and reality intermingle in recounting the life and times of the "half horse, half alligator" Kentuckians who guided those comfortless flatboats down the Kentucky, Ohio, and Mississippi Rivers to the southern Louisiana ports of Natchez and New Or-leans. Like the cowboy some 80 years later or Lawrence of Arabia

130 years later, journalists did not let facts interfere with a good story about heroes who were, in large part, creatures of their imagination. Journalists of a slightly later day portrayed these boatmen as romantic, freedom loving, swashbuckling, compelling heroes who were ready to place their lives on the line to move a large amount of goods and a few passengers to their appointed places. There may have been some who fit this mold, but not many.

The origin of the term "half horse, half alligator" as applied to all flatboatmen decending the Mississippi to New Orleans is obscure. Mike Fink, the most famous of the flatboatmen, may have applied it to himself or it may have been thrust upon him and his fellow boatmen by journalists of the early 19th century to depict the hard-drinking, lawless, crude, hard-fighting, and probably smelly men who debarked from flatboats in the lower Mississippi. Few to whom it was applied denied this label and the writers who romanticized them a half-century later used it to refer to flatboatmen in general, including those originating in the Kentucky River basin.

We do know, however, that all flatboats that reached these lower Mississippi ports were called "Kentucky Boats" and the men who got them there were called "Kentucky Boatmen"[11] no matter what their upstream origin. This may have been due to the very sketchy knowledge in the 1780's Spanish mind of the geography of the newly created United States in general and Kentucky in particular or the fact the first flotilla of boats to reach these ports was from Kentucky under General James Wilkerson. The emerging main-stem towns of the Ohio River such as Pittsburgh, Marietta (Ohio), Cincinnati, and Jeffersonville (Indiana) made major contributions to the flatboat trade as did the Ohio River tributaries comparable to the Kentucky River, such as the Allegheny, Monongahela, Muskingum, Scioto, Miami, Little Miami, and Wabash. For whatever reason, the name stuck, and the terms "Kentucky Boats" and "Kentucky Boatmen" were synonymous with all flatboats and their crews in the lower Mississippi until their demise in the mid-19th century.

To call a person a "Kentucky Boatman" was not necessarily a compliment. Proper Creole mothers of the late 18th century scolded their children with harsh French: "You, you're nothing but a filthy little Kentuckian." Their admonition was, however, somewhat justified. After one to three months on board these craft, facing constant life threatening dangers, living outside the entire time (most of which was in the winter), bad food and water, no sanitation facilities, plenty of whisky, and a few dollars in their pockets while in town, they were something less than the noble heroes they were, at a later time, portrayed to be.

Their life was filled with all of the dangers incumbent to late 18th and early 19th century land-dwelling frontiersmen: Indian attacks, disease, lack of food and proper water, life-threatening accidents, bandits, storms, bitter cold weather, and pistol or knife fights among themselves in addition to the perils peculiar to water, such as rapids, ice, hidden snags or rocks, sandbars, and leaky boats. If they reached their destination in the lower Mississippi, they were then faced with the major task of getting back home, if they had one. Signing on as a crew member of a keelboat was one option to go upstream, but most opted to walk the 1000 miles back to Kentucky. The backbreaking work of poling (pushing the boat upstream by poles thrust into the river bottom), cordelling (crew members on the bank pulling the boat upstream with a rope), or bushwhacking (pulling the boat upstream by pulling on overhanging bushes) a keelboat from New Orleans to Kentucky had little appeal to men who had just survived the downstream trip. The walk from New Orleans to Natchez was relatively safe as there was some habitation along this part of the route, but the Natchez Trace from Natchez to Nashville had its own set of hazards: bandits, swamps, biting insects, snakes, wild animals, rivers that had to be swam, and lack of food or water. Any illness along the way would likely mean death as there were no medical facilities, however crude, along the way.

The men who signed on to the flatboats were well aware of all of these dangers, but few of them had any other trade or source of livelihood. Many were of mixed blood, most could not read, and few came from anything resembling a stable home. The lifestyle they adapted on the flatboats was in line with the known dangers and their respective backgrounds.

The flatboats were totally devoid of all creature comforts. Some had nominal shelters, but this was for paying passengers, if any, or the merchant-captain. The crew slept in the open regardless of the weather. Since most of the downstream trips were in the winter when the water was high enough to float a boat and cold enough to preserve the meat products cargo, the weather was generally cold or wet or both. Cooking, when it was done, was generally on an individual basis or not at all. Some flatboats had a hearth and chimney, but most had only a sandbox area where the men would build a fire and cook pork or meat they had procured before leaving or from the cargo. The food was dull at best and decidely not healthy.

Whiskey, however, was in good supply for the entire voyage. It was intentionally served three times a day by the boatmaster and between times on an individual basis. Most cargos from Kentucky contained a few barrels of converted corn, which the crew tapped if and when the barrels designated for them became empty. The crew members were, therefore, in some degree of intoxication for most of the voyage. It might have been better for them that way, and the boat captains knew this. We know little of their conversation, but the passengers whose surviving journals of their voyages with them refer to the constant swearing and cursing of the crew members.

The lower Mississippi ports which were their principal destinations, Natchez and New Orleans, offered a catalog of every sin which any Bapist preacher's imagination could conjure: debauchery, carousing, sex for hire, drinking, smoking, swearing, fighting, gambling, dancing, robbery, and not infrequent murders. Even sleeping was dangerous as many Kentucky boatmen lay down for a night's rest, after engaging in as many sins as his few dollars would purchase, only to wake up to find himself robbed, in some gutter, and facing the long trip back home, on foot, penniless. The city fathers made half hearted attempts to curtail these activities, but realizing that the flatboat trade was the lifeblood of their respective cities, ended up isolating these sections of their cities from the eyes, ears, and noses of their more God-fearing citizens: the Swamp in New Orleans and Under-the-Hill in Natchez. These areas have been sanitized and glorified for the modern tourist, but in their day they contained little of either.

Because of the broad use of the term "Kentucky Boatman" in the lower Mississippi, from whence most of the documentation of the flatboat trade originates, it is hard to tell exactly how many flatboats came from the Kentucky River and who the crew members of them were. By most accounts they were young, single, and had a restless spirit. The journal of one Kentucky boatman noted that when he left for New Orleans, he: "Neither wept or was wept for." Some young men actually settled in the lower Mississippi as they had to declare during the Spanish days of the lower Mississippi, but most returned to Kentucky. There were probably a few slaves serving their masters as crew hands, but by the late 18th century and early 19th century when young men of English stock began to pour over the mountains, most of the names of Kentucky boatmen appear to be of this extraction. They were well used to the rigors of frontier life and saw this as one of their opportunities.

Ferries

The Kentucky River was both a blessing and a curse to the early settlers; it was an avenue of transportation within and without

Kentucky, and it was a major obstacle to cross much of the time. From the very beginning ferries across the river were the answer to this curse. At various times there were well over one hundred ferries chartered to cross the Kentucky River. Of these, only the ferry at Valley View, connecting Madison and Fayette/Jessamine counties, survives. It serves today the same vital service that it did when first chartered to John Craig in 1785: carrying passengers and cargo from one side of the river to the other.

In 1779 when the town of Boonesborough was still a toddler, the need for dependable service to get from one side of the river to the other was apparent. This town was the terminus of the Boone Trace and the point at which the trace on to Lexington crossed the river. Richard Callaway requested permission from the Virginia legislature to operate a public ferry from the Town Land to the land of the State since from the first seating of this town both the inhabitants and travelers had found it very inconvenient to cross the river only in dry seasons in the summer time and both this town and county had become very popular and much resorted by travelers.

The Virginia legislature quickly (for that day, since it took at least six weeks to travel to and from the Virginia capital, and the legislature may or may not be in session) granted this request which reads in part:[12]

> *Whereas it is represented to this present general assembly that public ferries at the places hereafter mentioned will be of great advantage to travelers and others; be it therefore enacted that public ferries be kept at the following places and the rates for passing same shall be as follows, ... at the town of Boonesborough in the County of Kentucky, across Kentucky River to the land on the opposite shore, the price for a man three shillings and for a horse the same; the keeping of which last mentioned ferry and the emolu-*

ments arising therefrom are given and granted to Richard Callaway, his heirs or assigns so long as he or they shall well and faithfully keep same according to the directions of this act; and for the transportation of wheel carriages, tobacco, cattle, and other beasts at the places aforesaid, the ferry-keeper may demand and take the following rates, that is to say, for every coach, chariot, or wagon, and the driver thereof, the same as for six horses, for every cart, or a four wheel chaise and the driver thereof the same as for four horses; for every two wheel chaise or chair, the same as for two horses: for every hogshead of tobacco, as for one horse, for every head of neat cattle as for one horse; for every sheep, goat, or lamb, one fifth part of the ferriage for one horse and for every hog one fourth part of the ferriage for one horse and no more.

Richard Callaway was killed by Indians while making a ferry boat. His sons operated the ferry after that.

The Act went on to state that a ferry keeper who demanded or received more than the legal rates must forfeit to the aggrieved party the ferriage and pay a fine of ten shillings. The chartering of this ferry was thus the first government-regulated utility or service west of the Allegheny Mountains. Many more have followed since. The purpose of the ferry charter and the established rate was to assure the ferry operator a fair return on his investment; and to protect the traveler against price gouging. The charter would give the operator confidence that a competing ferry would not open up next door, undercut his price and put him out of business. The Virginia legislature wanted to protect both the traveler and the ferry operator much like the present Public Service Commission operates today. The same general language was used to charter the many other ferries that followed: the place where they could operate and the fares they could charge.

When Kentucky became a state, the custom of regulating ferries continued, except that this power was assigned to county fiscal courts. The rates were fixed by the courts as well as the number of boats an operator could use and the number of "hands" he could employ at the site. The keeper of the ferry was a very important person to the economic life of a community and he was exempt from county taxes and duty on the county road maintenance labor crews, but he had to carry public messengers free. The court could also authorize him to operate a tavern at the ferry site, which most of them did. His rights to operate the ferry were forfeited if the ferry was in disuse for two years.

The operation of a ferry was a retail business, and like a retail business today, the first three things to consider were location, location, and location. The ferry had to have access from both sides of the river. A road, or at least the potential for a road, on both sides was a must. In the middle of the river, say the stretch from Frankfort to Boonesborough, the sides are lined with cliffs and a "pass" through these cliffs to the water's edge was a must if the ferry owner expected passengers and cargo to show up at his place. Then there must be some flat ground at the ferry landing for the various facilities that accompany a ferry, such as a tavern, warehouses, possibly stores, and, of course, a flat place for the ferry to load up on both sides of the river. The permanent structures such as the warehouses and tavern had to be out of the area that was subject to frequent floods, say every ten years, but the large floods that could rise as much as 35' to 38' would get everything wet. The most vital criterion was that the ferry had to be located where people and cargo were. The very early ones, say at Boonesborough and Mouth of Hickman, were located at early critical crossing points and probably operated several boats at one time. As the land filled up and goods were produced up and down the river, more ferries were opened to accommodate this need.

FERRIES

At various times there were more than one hundred ferries, much like these, operating on the Kentucky River. They were chartered first by the state then by the counties they served. Before the locks and dams, they were powered mainly by "poling" across the shallow river. After the locks and dams created deeper water, most of them pulled themselves across the river with a cable. Only the ferry at Valley View (Fayette, Jessamine, and Madison counties) remains today. A few of the others remained in use as late as WWII.

Evelyn Gate Ferry.

Typical hand-powered ferry. Cable can be seen at left end of the ferry.

*Valley View
Ferry in 2000.*

Valley View Ferry in 2000.

Paint Creek Ferry.

Before the locks and dams were built, the river could be forded some of the year, and this cut into the income of the ferry operator. James Hogan, for example, petitioned the county court for an increase in allowable fares because the river was fordable six months of the year and they paid him nothing. James Hogan must have done fairly well, though, as he leased his profitable ferry out to others and became a "gentleman farmer" on higher ground.

The ferry was the center of activity for the area it served. The complex almost always included warehouses (generally authorized by the county court for various goods, such as tobacco, hemp, flour, and other products), the tavern, general stores, and houses. As commerce developed, first with flatboats then steamboats, these river points became particularly important as passengers and goods from both sides of the river were funneled to that point. Substantial communities such as Valley View and Brooklyn sprang up at ferry landings, and some of these communities exist to this day. Frankfort, the only early town to develop on both sides of the river, was served by several ferries even after the first bridges were built; some of the early bridges fell into the river, and the town had to return to tried-and-true ferries, even though these were much slower than bridge crossings.

A variety of ways to propel the ferries across the river were used. Since about 1940, the Valley View ferry has been operating between two overhead cables, but this is not the way early ferries operated. Relatively little is known about the exact power mode of each ferry, but overhead cables across a navigable water-way was probably not one of them: they would have been in constant conflict with flatboat and steamboat traffic. The early ferries undoubtedly used oars, paddles, or poles to make the crossing. Some ferries used an underwater rope that could be pulled by hand across the boat. Small steam engines were used in places, but keeping fuel for them had to have been a problem. Some used horses or mules to turn a paddle or wheel.

As ferries began to die out, diesel and gasoline engines came into use, but this was shortlived.

The demise of the ferries was, of course, brought about by bridges and the automobile. The earliest bridges were at Frankfort and the Mouth of Hickman. Others soon followed and put the ferries out of business. Some ferries (other than Valley View) held on until after WWII, but these soon died out. There are no plans to replace the Valley View Ferry with a bridge. It is a national treasure.

The Three Forks

In the mountains of eastern Kentucky, from whence the Kentucky River springs above the three-forks area, the people, their life and culture was totally different from the downstream Bluegrass. The terrain is severe. Large farms are impossible. Land in the late 18th and early 19th centuries was cheap, running in pennies per acre if purchased in large tracks. It was closer, on the map, to mother Virginia, but few settlers came directly over the mountains to settle the three-forks area. Most of them came first to central Kentucky, then up the river to the cheap land, abundant game, and scarcity of civilization. They were a rugged lot, not given to the creature comforts of the Bluegrass and its emerging nobility. They sought their own way of life and wanted as little government interference as possible. In contrast to the Bluegrass area where the towns were built away from the river and its tributaries, the towns and settlements of the three-forks were built on the river banks, for there was no other place on which to build. There were a few settlers in the area prior to 1800, but the major upriver movement was from that date until 1820. The mountain area and the Bluegrass were really two separate countries bound together by a similar language.

The ownership of land was confusing from the beginning in eastern Kentucky. Treasury land warrants were issued for large tracts of public land at forty cents per acre to speculators, to land companies with some cash, and to absentee landlords. These land warrants were traded for goods and served as a sort of currency in the area. Some surveying was done and some of the surveyed land was registered, but there was a great deal of overlap of land ownership and different viewpoints of ownership of specific parcels were often settled with knives and pistols. As fear of Indian attacks lessened, inducements for Bluegrass settlers, who did not get as much land as they wanted, were issued by the holders of large tracts. A typical ad was placed in the Frankfort *Palladium* in 1805 for the sale of 18,000 acres of land:[13]

> " . . . *on the left-hand side of the Three-Forks as you go up the Kentucky and at their junction; running along the river three miles and nine miles back. The bottoms are rich land; the ridges are capable of producing small grain. The pasturage is excellent for raising stock of all kinds as it has plenty of cane breaks and vines. All along the river is the sugar tree, wild cherry and other woods common to this country. When you go back some distance is the pine which produces tar, turpentine, pitch, and rosin which will finally be valuable, independent of the wood that is upon the land.*
>
> *There is also a rock close to the low water mark, that when the water is very low shows clear salt upon its surface, and the rock itself tastes salt. There have been witches (as they call them) trying the experiment; they say there is four feet square of very salt water at the top of the bank which is not a hundred feet from the water; and close to it is a very easy ascending hill for several miles; and also the wood along the river.*

A coal bank is within three hundred yards. There are also five valuable coal banks near the river with easy access to them. Also a coal yard and a boat yard; and it is said several saltpetre caves. The bottoms and along the creek would produce good cotton and hemp, Lexington alone, independent of the country blacksmiths, consumes 13,000 bushels of coal per annum, and we will suppose Frankfort uses 5,000 bushels, which sells at the landing at one shilling per bushel; 20,000 bushels might be sold; this might be made productive by a man of small capital.

Independent of these advantages, the mouth of the three-forks is the best fishing place in the state. In a small crib they can get five hundred pounds of fish a day and may get by a seine five or seven hundred barrels per annum

Tobacco, flour, beef, pork, tallow, hog's lard, hemp, cordage, whiskey, or cast iron will be taken in payment for the land.

This ad is an early acknowledgment of coal as an exportable product, by the bushel. One can also but wonder how long the fish would have lasted if taken from the river at the rate noted in the glowing ad. It is evident also that hard currency was still in short supply in Kentucky in 1805.

Counties were created in eastern Kentucky, each with a county seat located on some tributary of the Kentucky River. Many of the county seats still have populations in the range of 2000 persons, and they were far smaller than this at the turn of the 19th century.

In the early days, the river was the only highway into the head-waters area. Indian hunting trails along the river banks were the only land trails into the region. During the winter rains and snows, these were virtually impassable. During the summer they were satisfactory for foot traffic, but heavy carts or wagons were beyond their capacity. Exportable agricultural products were out of the question in the mountains as the local population needed for survival all it could grow on the scarce flat river bottom land. There were exportable goods, however: salt, timber, iron, and coal. Coal, as a major factor, was not even a twinkle in the eyes of the very early eastern Kentucky settlers, but it would have more influence in the future development of the Kentucky River than all other goods put together.

Salt

In general, the land of eastern Kentucky is not suited for large farms or large crop yields. Virtually all of what was produced was consumed by the producing family or within the community. Little agricultural exports were made, but one commodity enjoyed a short, but vital life in downriver trade: salt. Within the three-forks area, a substantial number of salt springs surfaced, and some wells were ultimately bored into brine-bearing conglomerate formations. Salt is, of course, a vital element to any habitation, and finding it in marketable deposits on the frontier was especially important as it was the major preserver of meat as well as a generator of small amounts of hard currency when it was shipped to major downstream markets.

The early salt licks were located by trailing large animals as well as by assistance from the few friendly Indians. In the very early days of three-forks settlement, salt production was a "cottage" industry, using the utensils normally found in any frontier cabin to reduce the brine from a nearby spring to salt and trading the salt within the local area. Salt was then generally produced outdoors where attacks from Indians were a constant threat.

There also appears to be some price gouging by certain early salt producers. The preamble to an Act to supply the inhabitants of early Kentucky with salt upon reasonable terms began:[14]

> *Whereas, divers ill-disposed persons have possessed them-*
> *selves of large quantities of salt which they have not only*
> *refused to sell at any reasonable price, but to enhance the*
> *value of their own salt . . .*

An embargo was placed on certain shippers of salt, and free-holders might seize that salt upon warrant issued by a justice of the peace.

Enterprising settlers realized, however, that not everyone down-stream had access to a salt spring nor the energy to produce it. They began to import large copper kettles, made in West Liberty, Pennsylvania, which could produce salt on a commercial scale, using the abundant wood of the three-forks area as fuel. Salt springs and brine wells, major problems within the oil and gas industry today, were found in all three forks as well as the Red River basin. The salt was produced on a commercial basis year-round and shipped downstream when the river was sufficiently high. For many years the "wholesale" price was about one dollar per bushel at downstream landings, such as Lexington and Frankfort. The shipments were generally made in flatboats of fifty to sixty tons at some peril to both the crew and the salt, which had little tolerance to water. This trade did, however, influence the first improvement on the South Fork by the removal of some of the snags and rocks. The State Report of 1837-1839 gives the modern reader a sense of the difficulties of getting salt out of the three-forks area:[15]

> *It is necessary to navigate the Goose Creek by day on ac-*
> *count of the short bends and other obstacles to be avoided*
> *so that boats which leave the salt-works above Manchester*
> *arrive at the mouth of Red Bird in the evening, and are*
> *obliged to remain over night; but on the following morn-*
> *ing there is seldom water sufficient to pass the narrows*
> *and they are compelled to await another tide.*

It was the very strong feeling among the enterprising and relatively well-off producers and shippers of three-forks salt that a slackwater system into the area would greatly increase their business. The Board of Internal Improvement Report of 1836 states:[16]

> *The river is the principal channel for the conveyance of this salt to market. It is shipped in flatboats and sent down during winter and spring while the water is high to the country below. The delay and hazard connected with this kind of transportation operates against the interest of the manufacturer and limits the quantity of salt which he can produce. It is said if means of conveyance could be had at all seasons of the year at a moderate expense, that 400,000 to 600,000 bushels would be manufactured.*

It will never be known whether a slackwater system into the three-forks area would have saved the salt industry there, as slackwater to the three-forks area was still nearly a century away when these words were written. Salt did still remain a cash producer, on a gradually declining scale, until pre-Civil War times. Kentucky-three-forks area salt was slowly beaten out by other cheaper, more certain methods of production and transportation.

Brine today is considered a major enemy of the environment when it is encountered in drilling for oil and gas in eastern Kentucky. Scant thought is given to the early eastern Kentucky settlers who rejoiced in finding a convenient source of this vital material.

Iron

The production of iron, like the production of salt, in Kentucky is now all but forgotten, except by a handful of county historical societies. For a few brief years, however, it did appear that Kentucky would be a major iron producing state and that the Kentucky River would be the highway bringing coal to their furnaces and taking the iron to the world. In Estill, Powell, and Lee Counties, a brown hematite is found on top of the subcarboniferous limestone in commercially viable seams. Imlay's 1793 map of Kentucky shows a small settlement near Clay City (Powell County) that could have been the Clark and Smith forge for which an improvement to the Red River was made in 1805. The census of 1810 reported for Estill County, which then included Powell County, one forge valued at $10,000, with a product of eighty tons and one furnace.

Several furnaces were set up in these counties and were major factors to the local economy through the Civil War period and peaked out at about 1870-1874. The Kentucky River carried most of the iron to downstream markets in flatboats of about eighty tons capacity. Local ore was brought to the furnaces mainly by wagon, with wood as the principal energy source for their firing.

The demise of the iron industry was brought about by several unrelated reasons: crude, inefficient methods of mining the iron ore; a tax imposed on cargo going down the Kentucky River; and the exhaustion of timber to fuel the furnaces. The poor condition of the Kentucky River also contributed to the death of the iron industry in Kentucky. The State Geological Survey of 1876 states:[17]

> *Iron can be produced at these furnaces for much less than at many other localities which are nearer to market, as ore, labor, and charcoal are all cheap; but the facilities for transportation are so poor that it costs from seven to ten dollars per ton to carry the iron from the furnace to market at Louisville or Cincinnati. This tax is so great at present prices, it either entirely consumes the profits or leaves the margin so small that it is not worth the risk . . .Were there a railroad or slack-water transportation within a few miles of each furnace it would be profitable to make iron in this region, even at the present extremely low prices, but the*

IRON PRODUCTION IN KENTUCKY

From 1791 until 1874 Kentucky was a substantial producer of iron with furnaces in Estill, Lee, and Powell counties. The iron was made in the Kentucky River basin and shipped down river by barge. Both the iron ore and the wood to fire the furnaces soon gave out and the furnaces turned cold. These furnaces shown in these photos are in Estill County in the Red River basin. Clockwise they are the Cottage Furnace (built in 1856), the Fitchburg Furnace (operated between 1869 and 1874) and the Estill Steam Furnace (operated between 1830 and 1874).

Bill Grier

necessity of wagoning it great distances or of awaiting the uncertain rises of the Kentucky River and the dangers of navigation when the rises come renders the cost of transportation entirely too great.

By 1874 iron production in the Kentucky River headwaters had ended, but there was still a strong belief that a viable Kentucky River (to the three-forks) would stimulate the economic life of eastern Kentucky. This concept was reinforced by information disseminated from the State Geological Survey.

Logging and Timber

Kentucky has long been a political "border" state, and the natural forest cover of eastern Kentucky follows this characteristic. Southern pine and magnolia grow side by side with northern hardwoods and shrubs with an all-regions mix between. The word "diversity" best explains the forest cover of the upper Kentucky River basin. When the first longhunters crossed the Appalachian Mountains, all of the Kentucky River headwaters were a giant forest with white oak, chestnut oak, beech, chestnut, yellow poplar, black oak, and walnut being the most commercially important species. Neither the Indians nor the early settlers were good stewards of the land and treated the forest as though it had no end. Dr. Thomas Walker writes in 1750, probably on Station Camp Creek (Jackson County), *The woods have been burnt some years past and are now very thin, the timber being almost killed.* Probably from the banks of the Red River he writes: *The woods are burnt fresh about here and are the only fresh burnt woods we have seen these six weeks.* Apparently Dr. Walker saw both virgin and destroyed forests.

Indian and white hunters alike used the barbarous method of fire-hunting, especially for deer. The Virginia Assembly in 1738 passed a law for the *better preservation of the breed of deer.* The preamble to the Act reads, in part: *and it is also found by experience, that this making large circles and setting the same on fire round the converts where the deer usually lodge called fire hunting is not only destructive to the breed of deer but also to the young timber and food of the cattle.* When the settlers came in the early 19th century to stay and farm, the forest was viewed much more of a hindrance than an asset and they destroyed the trees as best they could to make way for their fields. Virtually everything was made of solid wood, and lots of it. Their log cabins, of a few hundred square feet in size, for example, used more wood than a modern house several times the size, because cabin walls were solid wood while in a modern house the walls are basically hollow. Wood was the only structural material available and was used on a massive scale. Six or eight inch square timbers were common in industrial construction with no effort to save the part of a tree that was not in the timber. There was no need to; there was plenty more where that came from, and it was more trouble to get two side-by-side timbers from a log than one.

In spite of the exploitation of the forest, there were many good trees left standing, particularly on the mountain slopes where farming could not be done and were out of easy reach of early settlers. Serious logging for downstream mills began about 1835. The earliest trees to be harvested were those along the shore of the main stem where they could easily be floated downstream with relatively little effort to get them to water. Quality logs along the main stem were soon exhausted, and the logging moved upstream to the heads of the hollows, where the creeks are often little more than a trickle.

Logging began after the fall harvest and lasted until spring planting. This was done not only because of the availability of farm labor during the winter, but also because it was easier to snake a log out of the woods when the vegetation was less and the ground often frozen. The felled trees were cut into proper lengths, branded as to the owner, and dragged or hauled by mule or oxen to the nearest stream where they were piled to await a "tide' to carry them downstream. In very small streams that would never have enough water to float them downstream, the logs, together with earth and other material, were piled in a fashion to form a "splash dam" that would impound water behind it and had a "key wedge" that could be pulled, thereby pulling the dam down, releasing the impounded water behind it and carrying all the logs downstream where they were rafted or passed on downstream singly.

Before real commercial traffic on the upper river began, the logs were floated individually downstream and removed by log booms at the sawmills. "Out-of-control" floating of logs down the river posed something of a hazard to boating, and the producers were compelled by force of law to form them into rafts, which were somewhat controlled by one or two oarsmen. The rafts on the main stem were about 15' to 20' wide and 60' to 100' long, containing about 15,000 to 20,000 board feet of timber. Rafts formed on the smaller tributaries were about one half that size due to the narrow banks. Oarsmen received two dollars a day wages plus expenses for the five day run between Beattyville and Frankfort, where the early mills were located. Expenses while on a log raft were probably not great. The floating speed was about four miles per hour and only daylight travel was possible. The walk back to Beattyville required about two and one half days.

Before the advent of steam-driven sawmills in the early 1800's, sawmills for major timber cutting did not exist. Lumber was cut by hand or with crude animal or water-powered saws near where the tree was felled. Steam-driven machinery first came to the larger towns and the early sawmills were therefore located in Frankfort and Louisville where the logs could be taken directly out of the river. Steam power permitted the cutting of relatively large quantities of lumber with relatively few hands. The railroads, not the turbulence of a river, were needed to carry cut lumber from the sawmill to the lumberyard, and the railroads in Frankfort and Louisville served this purpose well before they were extended into the three-forks area. As steam machinery, and ultimately railroads, reached the three-forks area, sawmills of considerable size were built in Irvine, Beattyville and Jackson. Massive holding ponds were built, and logs were funneled into them by the log booms stretched across the river.

LOGGING ON THE KENTUCKY RIVER

These photos from old postcards show the extent of logging on the Kentucky at its prime. The date of these photos is not known, but it is apparent that logging activity was very high. The log booms and the men operating them are in evidence in these photos.

Logging on Kentucky River, Kentucky.

Clyde Bunch

Clyde Bunch

Logging on the Kentucky River.

Log booms, which are essentially a line of logs strung by a cable stretched across the river to divert the floating logs into the holding pond, work well under moderate water conditions. When the flow is high, the logs can pass over the boom or are moving so fast that it is difficult to divert them into the holding pond. Sudden bursts of rainfall in the headwaters can instantaneously release thousands of logs at one time from the splash ponds and piles built up during the past several months causing a massive buildup on the booms. In Jackson, for example, preachers, lawyers, bankers, and prominent business men were pressed into service to man the booms as thousands of logs per hour entered the booms following an upstream cloudburst, as reported in the local paper. The paper did not mention, however, how well these Jackson elite performed their duties on the log booms, but it is reasonable to assume that some of them, at least, had risen from more earthy stock and knew well the feel of dirt beneath their fingernails.

The reverse of this occurred during an extended drought when no logs could be floated and the mills were forced to shut down for lack of supply.

Not all of the logs ever made it to market: floods carried them past the log booms; they became crushed in the booms; ice hindered their movement; they stayed upstream for several years waiting a major rainfall to take them down; or they just became waterlogged and sunk. At least ten percent of the logs were assumed to be lost. Some thoughts of recovering these "lost" logs are being examined today to determine if they can be marketed. (If wood stays constantly wet and not exposed to air, it will remain solid for a very long period of time.)

The heyday of logging in the Kentucky River basin was also the heyday of railroad building in Kentucky as well as nationwide. A large quantity of the logs was converted into rail ties. The best ones (walnut, white and chestnut oak) were hand-hewed by the landowner and sold directly to the railroad companies. With this process, a single tie per cut (tree diameter) could be made while larger trees could produce two ties per cut if machine cut.

Despoliation of the forests of the Kentucky River basin was the chief contributor to the demise of the logging industry of the headwaters area. No effort of any kind was made by the foresters to restore the trees they removed, and the techniques to remove trees from the mountain slopes destroyed what was left of the young trees that could one day be harvested. Before the turn of the 20th century the state paid little attention to forest care; hence, most of the prime timber of the Kentucky River basin was gone by that time. The mindset that forest would be endless was still dominant in much of Frankfort bureaucracy . In 1906, however, the Kentucky Legislature added a Department of Forestry to the Board of Agriculture. In 1907 this board asked for and received a $2,000 appropriation from the Federal Forest Service for work toward forest restoration, and positive action was begun to this end.

The development of the slackwater system to the three-forks area, which was completed in 1917, together with the construction of the railroads, rang the death knell of water-moved timber, or what little was left. Logs could no longer float freely downstream. The log rafts had to be locked through just like any other craft. During high water they could sometimes ride over the dams, but this was at some hazard to the oarsmen on them. The locking operation could take up to one half hour for each lockage, and if there were a number of rafts waiting to be locked through, a considerable time delay could be experienced.

The advent of the railroads into the three-forks eliminated most need for water transportation of logs out of the headwaters. By this point in time the logs were at least rough cut in the mountains before shipment out. The railroads were now the carriers of outbound lumber.

Coal

Kentucky coal was first brought to the attention of the outside world by Christopher Gist during his 1750 explorations for a development company in Virginia. Little note was taken of his findings. The outcroppings of coal were evident to the early settlers, but wood was still their fuel of choice. Wood was a familiar fuel, light weight, found in abundance, and did not burn at a particularly high temperature. As the eastern Kentucky settlers gained some degree of permanence, coal began to be used in fireplaces and blacksmith shops.

Coal outcroppings in the Kentucky River headwaters area were very widespread. At first a settler or farmer would extract coal from an outcropping on his land for his or his extended family's domestic use. This gradually expanded to the creation of limited "mines," which extended 50' to 75' into the hillside, or as far as the farmer deemed safe from collapse. "Farmers" who showed special skills at coal extraction began to do this on a full time basis and deliver coal within his immediate community in a wagon. The price of coal was quoted by the "bushel," which in the early days was less than $0.10 per bushel, delivered. The local blacksmith was the only commercial user of early coal. Small but not extensive shipments outside the immediate communities began around 1800 to Frankfort area blacksmiths. It was also noted by an 1807 traveler to Kentucky that coal heated the penitentiary in Frankfort. Extensive use outside the immediate producing community was out of the question because neither the wagons nor the roads could bear that much weight. Major use of coal by steam engines and iron production was not in sight at this time.

A pound of coal has several times the heat content of a pound of even the best wood, and the Lexington and Frankfort fireplaces were beginning to convert to this fuel. By 1835 about 75,000 bushels (3,000 tons) were shipped from the three-forks area to the Lexington and Frankfort markets by barge. The coal was taken from the easiest outcroppings along the streams where it could be loaded directly onto a barge for downstream shipment. The North Fork between Jackson and Hazard was the earliest major producer with the Middle and South Forks producing mainly for their local markets. The report of the Board of Internal Improvement for 1835-36 states:[18]

> *The principal veins that are now mined and which but ineffectually supply the markets of Lexington and Frankfort are near the mouth of South Fork (Beattyville); near the mouth of Troublesome Creek, sixty miles up North Fork where it is found in better quality than in any other part of the United States; and near Perry County Courthouse (Hazard), fifty miles higher up the same fork.*

The "ineffectual supply" noted above was due to the very ineffectual methods of extracting the coal from the seams and the even more ineffectual methods of shipping it downstream. Coal removal techniques were little removed from the methods used by "digger farmers" of the frontier days. Shallow tunnels less than one hundred feet were extended into an exposed "drift" as close as possible to the water's edge and loaded directly onto the waiting barge. No props or ventilation were used in the shallow tunnels. When it appeared unsafe to go further into the hillside, a new pit was opened. The barges were floated on the small, natural pools created by the sandbars to await a winter or spring "tide" to carry them downstream. Barges loaded in the summer or fall had to sit, loaded, in the shallow water all winter waiting this tide. Sudden unexpected downpours could break the barges loose and dash several days labor upon the rocks below. Once floating downstream, there were still the sandbars, rocks, and snags that could sink the heavily loaded, but flimsy, leaky barges built for a single down-stream trip.

Mining and hauling difficulties notwithstanding, coal was (and is) the major hard currency generator in the headwaters area. The entrepreneurs engaged in this trade were still small businessmen, but their hands held a very high card: Kentucky River coal was (and is) recognized as some of the best in the world. On every market, Kentucky River coal commanded a premium price. It has high heat content, low sulfur, and low ash content. Marketing coal still presented some problems to this emerging market. There were no repositories for coal storage along the river, and whenever a coal barge showed up in Lexington or Frankfort, the coal had to be sold at the spot market of that moment. When the river was high and barges were coming frequently, the price would drop. During low flow periods, no coal at all was delivered to Lexington or Frankfort. This problem was never fully worked out. It was voided by other events.

Events were stirring in Frankfort in the 1830's that were intended to aid the coal fields of the three-forks area, but ended in their near devastation. The coal-county politicians and businessmen, who knew that the shipment of coal down the Kentucky River was uncertain at best, held that the creation of slackwater all the way to the three-forks area would permit unlimited quantities of Kentucky coal to reach the world market. They knew well the high value of Kentucky River coal and brought to bear every pressure at their disposal upon Frankfort to create a water highway to the three-forks to get it out. Water transportation was still understood to be the only method to move bulky cargo as railroads were in their infancy and none were even on the drawing board for the three-forks area where the coal was.

The Frankfort hierarchy responded to their pleas, and possibly with other motives in mind, with the construction of five flimsy dams, with stable locks, that created slackwater from the Ohio River past Frankfort. When these were completed in 1842, the state treasury was completely broke, and slackwater could be extended no further. The three-forks area was still 166 miles and nine dams away, but Frankfort had a year-round slackwater river to the world. The effect of this was that coal mined in Pennsylvania could be more cheaply floated down the Ohio River then up the Kentucky to Frankfort than the seasonal shipments of coal down the Kentucky River could be made. The production of coal in the three-forks area took a thorough drubbing from Pennsylvania coal, and the mines began to close.

The 1875 report by the Kentucky Geological Survey on this matter had a more long-range effect upon the development of the Kentucky River than any other report before or since. The key parts are:[19]

> *There are numerous mines along the Kentucky River where coal has been mined for shipment in boats down the river, but none of these are extensive and the majority are now abandoned and have fallen in . . . . . .*

> *Of late years, owing to the price of coal in the lower markets, coal mining has not been as profitable as formerly and but little is now mined in this region, except the finer grades of cannel coal which brings a higher price and can, therefore, yet be mined and transported at a profit . . . . .*

> *The cause of this stagnation in the mining industry is the excessive cost of transportation due entirely to the uncertainty and danger of river navigation. Coal boats drawing five feet of water can only be run during high water which can be expected but a very small portion of the year. This,*

therefore, necessitates the storage of large quantities of coal, often for months after it is mined, while waiting for a rise in the river sufficient to carry it off . . . .

In addition to the injury and loss by exposure, an extra cost is involved through the loss of capital lying idle for so long a time. The boats used to carry the coal down the river can never be returned and they are usually sold at a great loss. The river is so difficult of navigation that from three to five men are required to manage each boat, or one man to about each thousand bushels of coal, the boats usually holding from three to five thousands bushels of coal each. In addition to these necessary and inevitable expenses, there is a great risk involved in the navigation of the river, a large proportion of the boats never reaching their destination.

These combined causes make the cost of coal at the markets along the Ohio River so great that Pennsylvania coal is brought down the Ohio River and up the Kentucky and sold at less in Frankfort than coal from this region. Thus the work which has been done by the State in improving the navigation of the Kentucky River for a part of its course only, actually operates against the interests of Kentucky coal miners instead of furthering them, for it enables the Pennsylvania coal to compete with them in their own markets without assisting them in any degree.

Were the Kentucky slack-watered to the mines, so that coal could be shipped at nearly all seasons of the year and the empty barges returned cheaply, this region could supply coal to the whole of that part of the State bordering the

*river at prices which would drive all foreign coal from the
market; and it could even do a large business on the Ohio
River in the fine cannel coals in which it abounds. Until
improved means of transportation are furnished this region, either by slackwater or railroad, there can be no extensive and regularly conducted mining enterprises. The
fine cannel coals will probably continue to be mined in a
precarious and haphazard way as they commonly bring a
price sufficient to pay a small profit over the risk and expense of transportation, but with this exception, the great
body of coal will remain untouched.*

These words from the highly respected Kentucky Geological
Survey, backed by the urgings of the mountain political forces, ultimately brought a slackwater system to the three-forks area, some
42 years after these words were written. By that time the need for
a slackwater system to the coal mines had long since passed as the
railroads had built an extensive system throughout the Kentucky
River headwaters region that could handle coal in far greater quantities cheaper, quicker, and safer than a chain of locks and dams
could possibly do. The need to move salt and iron downstream, as
once thought, had likewise long passed.

The slackwater system so forcefully requested by the Kentucky
Geological Survey does, however, supply an economic foundation
to a much greater area than ever visioned in 1875.

The Dawn of Steam

The use of steam power drove the industrial revolution and
had a likewise driving force upon the development of the Kentucky River.

Little is recorded in history books about Kentucky's early brush
with the development of steam. John Fitch, an inventor, settled in

Bardstown, Nelson County, Kentucky in 1780 where he built a model of a steamboat. Since Kentucky did not become a state until 1792 and had a population of about one person per square mile, the time was not ripe for commercial steam traffic on its waters, hence Fitch relocated to the Delaware River in eastern Pennsylvania to further his work. He petitioned Congress for funds to develop a commercial steam boat and obtained from the legislatures of Pennsylvania, New Jersey, New York, and Delaware the exclusive right to navigate certain waters with boats powered by steam. In the late 1780's he successfully operated a commercial steamboat on the Delaware River powered with a system of cranks and paddles. Congress granted him a patent for his invention in 1791, but he failed to obtain financial backing for the commercial devel-

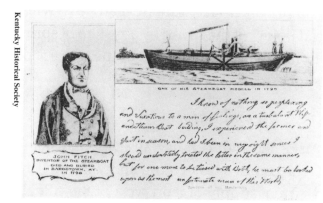

JOHN FITCH

John Fitch is probably the real inventor of the steamboat, the device which completely revolutionized navigation.

Fitch developed his first steamboat model in Kentucky in 1780, but saw the real need for steam boats was in the northeast. His first operational model was on the Delaware River which operated with a system of cranks and paddles. He failed to secure financial backing for this enterprise and returned to Kentucky where he apparently committed suicide with drugs.

The note, in Fitch's handwriting, "I know of nothing so perplexing and vexatious to a man of feeling, as a turbulant Wife and steam boat building. I have experienced the former and last in season, and had I been in my right senses I should have treated the latter in the same manner, but for one man to be teased with Both, he must be looked upon as the most unfortunate man of this World".

opment of his invention, which would ultimately revolutionize travel, industry, and commerce.

Discouraged and despondent, Fitch returned to Kentucky to seek financial backing there, but found instead an effort to take away the land he had claimed in Nelson County. His land claims were successfully defended, but his failure as an inventor reduced him to drink and do drugs and he apparently committed suicide with an overdose of both in 1789. The model of a boat left by Fitch to a friend in Bardstown was destroyed by fire in 1805. The steamboats patented by Robert Livingston and Robert Fulton, with whom history credits the invention of the steamboat, were essentially the same as the patent granted earlier to Fitch.

Robert West successfully operated a model steamboat on Town Branch in Lexington in 1794. His model had no flywheel, but overcame the "dead point" of the stroke by a system of springs. A patent was issued for his invention in 1802, but the concept of a flywheel emerged as superior.

Western Rivers Steamboats

At the turn of the 19th century all eyes, and many feet, were turned west. The country was young and vigorous and there was an unlimited virtual supply of land west of the Allegheny Mountains, or so people thought. The west is responsible for the development of many things typically American: the six shooter, the windmill, the covered wagon, barbed wire, and the western river steamboat. The steamboat was first developed on the eastern seaboard where there were money, people, and deep water. The west in the early 19th century had none of these, but getting people and goods around in the vast empty west, an area much larger than Europe, gave the world a unique water vessel: the western rivers steamboat. The "western rivers" is simply another name for the Mississippi River basin, of which the Kentucky River is a small part. It included all of the area from New Orleans north to the Canadian border, west to Great Falls, Montana and Denver Colorado, and east to New York state and Whitesburg, Kentucky. These rivers bear names that stir men's souls, such as the Missouri, the Yellowstone, the De Moines, the Red, the White, the Ohio, and the Tennessee Rivers. All are part of this giant system. These rivers had many features in common, and it took a very special steamer to serve them. Such was the western rivers steamer.

The features these rivers had in common were they were shallow much of the time, very deep some of the time, had an abundance of snags (large fallen trees), had few waves, were generally protected from high winds, were not suitable for fixed docks, required frequent stops to move people and goods, flowed through remote areas, and had a reasonably good supply of rapids. The first steamboats built on the eastern seaboard were basically sailing ship hulls with a steam engine in them. These ships, many of which had keels several feet below the bottom of a deep hull to provide stability in high seas, simply would not fit on western waters. They could go a short distance up the main stem of the Mississippi, but no farther. From this need, the very small-draft western river boat evolved and served countless towns, cities, plantations, factories, and farmers along the thousands of miles of western rivers for the hundred years between 1820 and about 1920. The Kentucky River was a typical tributary of this vast river system that led to New Orleans.

Well into the latter part of the 19th century, steamboats were built by craftsmen rather than by engineers who would carefully calculate buoyancy, center of gravity, skin friction, and other things engineers calculate. The western rivers steamer was the result of trial and error on the part of the boat owner, who generally had a heavy hand in the building of "his" boat, and the boat builder. The life expectancy of a western river steamer was very short, compared to its eastern seaboard cousins; hence, a boat owner and a builder had ample opportunity to put new ideas into practice.

The hulls of steamers and sailing craft used on eastern waters and on the ocean were built to withstand high seas and waves in deep water. Western waters had no high seas, no waves, and no deep water most of the time. The change of the hull design from a deep "V" to a very flat and low structure was the first major departure from conventional ship design. By drawing only a few feet of water, the hull had to displace a sufficient weight of water to float it. In the absence of a keel, the center of gravity of the boat had to be very low to keep it from capsizing. The hull all but disappeared from view. The western rivers boat sailed "on" the water rather than "in" it as its ocean-going relatives did. As the trial and error design process took place from 1827 to 1880, the draft of a 400+ ton steamer dropped from around 10' to about 6', a large change in rivers where a few inches of water mattered. The first five locks on the Kentucky River, built from 1836-1842, were 38'x145' with a draft of 6-feet sized for a 200 ton steamer. By the year 1880, the draft of a 200 ton steamer was reduced to about 5', but due to the use of lighter materials in the superstructure the dimensions of the hull of a 200 ton steamer were increased to more than 150 feet and would not fit into these locks. Soon after the locks were placed into operation, the boats that could pass through them were limited in their capacity by the length and width of the lock chambers but not by their draft.

The design of the hull also had to accommodate the absence of fixed wharves or docks for the transfer of goods and people. Many of the stops on the Kentucky were merely major farm landings where the construction of docks would have been impossible and the water level in the river fluctuated many feet in elevation between the wet and dry seasons. Fixed docks would have been of no value, and floating docks would have been impossible to access from the land in high water. This problem was solved by giving the bow of the vessel a long rake, that is, an overhang. The vessel would nose into the bank with its bow overhanging the shore and push into the mud a little. The gangplank was let down from the bow to the shore for the transit of people and goods. If needed, the paddles were kept slowly turning to offset the effect of currents.

The superstructure, or the part of the boat above the hull, was crucial to the financial success of the boat. It carried the freight, the passengers, the crew, and the machinery, but it was dead weight and every effort was made to reduce its weight to make room for paying cargo or passengers without increasing the all-important draft of the hull. Lighter materials were used that could offer the same strength at reduced weight. A shift from oak to lighter poplar, white pine, and cedar was made for the decking, but not the hull itself. The *Isaac Shelby*, built specifically for the Kentucky River trade at 120 tons, boasted a draft of only eleven inches without cargo. Operating on the Kentucky and other shallow western waters became a source of pride and display of humor of some of the captains. One owner, whose boat could operate in eight inches of water without cargo, mounted a sprinkler can on the bow of the boat to show that she could supply her own water if needed. Other captains boasted that they could walk ahead of their boat, with a lantern, to pick out the channel while others spoke of the heavy dew upon which they could sail. George Fitch, an early western boat builder, wrote that a steamboat *must be so built that when the river is so low and the sandbars come out of the air, the first mate can tap a keg of beer and run the boat four miles on the suds.* There is no record that this actually took place, but it probably came up. The success of steamboats on the Kentucky River, prior to the lock/dam system was a result of small tonnage and small drafts. When the river depth would not permit cargo on a boat, passengers could still be transported. The boat owners had to prove they could keep on schedule. Shippers forgave them if nature did not supply enough water to float their cargo.

Nineteenth-century settlers moving west in covered wagons spent their campfire evenings discussing the relative merits of mules versus oxen to pull their wagons. There was valid argument on both sides as each beast had strong and weak points. A similar argument took place between boat owners over the use of side wheelers versus a single stern wheel. They were both paddles built upon an axis or shaft powered by a steam engine, but the similarity ended there. All of the early riverboats had side wheels. These wheels gave better stability from rocking in the water, they kept the large weight of the wheels near the center of the craft, they provided better handling characteristics in the water, and ultimately they could move independently of each other when two steam engines were used. The biggest argument in their favor, however, was the way a riverboat was supposed to look.

One of the major arguments in favor of the stern wheel was that its position in the rear of the vessel protected it from floating debris and snags, which were very common on the Kentucky and most other western rivers. Repair to the paddles was much less frequent to stern wheelers than to side wheelers. A stern wheeler could operate in much smaller streams by virtue of a more narrow width and needed less draft in which to function. A stern wheeler was decidedly slower than a side wheeler, but it could operate longer in the year and carry more cargo as the rear paddles did not move down as more cargo was added. Because side wheels came first, old-time river captains looked down their noses at stern wheelers, regarding them with contempt. From their point of view, these crafts were fit for only menial tasks and the meaner kinds of work, not fit company for the majestic side wheelers.

Prior to the Civil War, the proportion of side wheelers versus stern wheelers changed from time to time and place to place on western waters. The shallow depth of the Kentucky River and ultimately the size of the lock chambers decided which was suitable for the Kentucky River: the stern wheeler. After the Civil War, technical innovations were made, particularly with regard to steering and handling, that favored the more economical stern wheeler. By that time, freight that had to move fast was moved by rail, but if freight economics was the factor of choice, the stern wheeler had the edge. The side wheeler remains today, however, as the classic profile of a riverboat.

Of all the factors affecting steam boats, none compared to the steam engine itself. Until well after the Civil War there were only three kinds of non-human/animal power to drive industry and transportation: steam power, water power, wind power. The steam engine, by far, dominated and drove the industrial revolution on both land and water, and it was the steam engine that drove the development of the Kentucky River.

The development of the steam engine on western waters was separate from the development of other forms of steam power as its use and application was unique to these waters. A compact, lightweight, powerful, dependable engine was needed to move cargo and people through the shallow western waters. This craft ventured far beyond the reach of major repair shops, and when "something went wrong," a local machine shop or foundry had to be able to fix it. The steam engines built on the eastern seaboard did not meet these specifications; hence, there emerged a unique form of steam power suitable for western waters. Names that live in the history books, such as Watt, Fulton and Shreve, indeed had their hand in the development of the western waters steam engine, but the real credit for this unique device lies with shop foremen, craftsmen, and master mechanics who are found in no history books, hung few diplomas upon their walls, but possessed minds and hands that grasped both problems and solutions.

The very early steam engines (prior to 1804) were built in the east, but after this date three major centers of western waters steam engine construction emerged: Pittsburgh, Cincinnati, and Louisville. The very early steam engines were "low pressure," that is pressure in the 10-12 pounds per square inch (psi) range. Much of the power of this type of engine was from condensing the steam on the discharge side of the stroke with a jet of cold water. This created a vacuum that enhanced the pressure of the steam itself. The major advantage of this type of engine was thinner boiler plates, hence less damage when they exploded (which they did). The condensed boiler water was also recirculated. Their major disadvantages were a bulky piece of machinery, with cylinders up to 36 inches in diameter to yield any power at all, and the complexity of the condensing mechanism.

Pressure and boiler plate integrity gradually increased beginning about 1814, and by 1825 virtually all steam engines built for western waters were for high-pressure steam, which at that time was up to about 120 psi. Some of the more hardheaded boat owners clung to the low-pressure engines, but competition soon drove them from the water. High-pressure engines had no condensing features and simply discharged their exhaust steam into the atmosphere, hence used more fuel than low pressure models. To the wood-rich west, fuel conservation was of little concern and the high pressure engine had much better "reserve" power; that is, it could respond to the need for a burst of power. Ascending western water rapids required a burst of power as did maneuvering around the frequent snags and rock outcrops. The limiting power of a steam engine was, and still is, the strength of the boilers. A boiler rated at 120 psi was often pushed to 160 psi, but this was tops.

To the eye, the configuration of the steam engine was the major change in its evolution. The very early steam engines used the "walking beam" or the "grasshopper" configuration in which a vertical cylinder moved a horizontal beam up and down on its central axis. The horizontal beam was 15' to 20' in the air, had a very high center of gravity, consumed large space, and was totally unsuited to western waters. This gangling arrangement quickly gave way to a horizontal cylinder in which the piston rod was connected directly to a crank turning the paddle wheel(s). This, together with the shape of the hull, was probably the major contribution of western waters to the development of steam power. All of the major problems of the vertical cylinder were overcome by this arrangement, and after about 1817 horizontal cylinders were all that were used in western waters.

Other improvements were continually made to the mechanics of the western rivers steam engine, generally by the master mechanics, craftsmen, and boat owners and without the benefit of the patent office. From the early 1830's until the turn of the century, the basic western steam engine remained unchanged.

Kentucky River Steamers - 1818-1842

The exact date of the first steamboat on the Kentucky River is somewhat unclear. Frankfort was a minor boatbuilding center in the very early 1800's, and an 1807 traveler noted that three "brigs" had been built above the bridge in Frankfort and sent down the Ohio and Mississippi Rivers. According to the *Navigator*, an inland waterway trade journal of that day, a number of "vessels of burden" were constructed in Frankfort in 1810 and had been "freighted" with produce of the Bluegrass to "New Orleans and West India Islands, etc." These accounts did not specifically mention steam power, but they well may have been. Also in 1810 the *Navigator* refers to *"A steamboat — that is a large boat to be propelled by the power of steam — was on the stocks a little above town. She is intended for the trade of the Ohio and Mississippi Rivers."*

The first recorded steamboat voyage on the Kentucky River was on April 28, 1816, when a steamboat made by Bosworth and West departed from the mouth of Hickman Creek bound for New Orleans. Based on an editorial notice in the *Kentucky Gazette*, this vessel appears to have been built according to Mr. West's spring design (rather than the flywheel):[20]

> *This boat was upon a plan distinct from any other steamboat then in use, and on a trial against the current of the Kentucky River at a high stage more than answered the sanguine expectations of her owners (a company of Lexington gentlemen) and left no doubt that she could stem the current of the Mississippi with rapidity and ease.*

She did not return. If the boat made it as far as New Orleans, it is possible that it was confiscated as Robert Livingston's permission was needed to permit a steamer to navigate Louisiana waters where Livingston had extensive political influence. This was the period of the fierce monopoly wars by Livingston and Fulton. They were attempting to obtain monopolies for steamboat operation on such far-ranging rivers as the Ganges, Thames, and the St. Petersburg-Kronstadt run in Russia. For them a monopoly in Louisiana was a cinch. When they petitioned the hard-nosed Kentucky legislature for a 20-year steamboat monopoly on its waters, the committee prudently denied the request: *It would . . . . be dangerous and impolitic to invest a man or set of men with the sole power of cramping, controlling, or directing the most considerable part of the commerce of the country for so great a period.*[21]

The first regularly scheduled operation was established in 1818 with the steamer *Kentucky* between Frankfort and Louisville. The schedule was regular, provided one wanted to travel when the water in the Kentucky River was high enough to float a steamer. Other steamers were constructed, and it is possible that as early as 1820 regular (high water) runs were scheduled between Frankfort and New Orleans. The May 3, 1820, *Kentucky Reporter* contained an ad for through freight by steamer to New Orleans:[22]

> *On the first rise of water in the Kentucky River the steam-*
> *boat Providence will leave Leestown one mile below Frank-*
> *fort for New Orleans. Independent of the freight I shall put*
> *on board the steamboat she will be able to carry from 150*
> *to 200 tons. Any person having property at a place they*
> *wish shipped to New Orleans will have an opportunity of*
> *freighting it in the above boat. etc.*

The August 23, 1820, issue of the *Reporter* advertised for sale: "New Orleans goods" received by the steamer *Fayette*. It was evident that two-way commerce was established between Kentucky and New Orleans.

The advent of passenger steamboats changed the basic concept of the river use and much of the life of middle and upper-class Kentuckians. Travel in rural Kentucky in the early 19th century was anything but comfortable, quick, and cheap. Rural roads were little more than dust trails when the weather was dry and mud trails when the weather was wet. Railroads were not yet on the Kentucky horizon, and travel beyond one's county line by carriage or horseback was done only with considerable thought and expense, provided one was not in a hurry to get anywhere. With the advent of the steamer, passengers could now go up and down the river to the major cities of Louisville, Cincinnati, St. Louis, or New Orleans in comfort and speed undreamed of prior to steam power. Frankfort legislators could now leave town in a hurry, if needed, provided this need arose during high water. Freight could be delivered on time, both ways, during high water. Finished goods could be protected from the weather during transit. Boat crews did not have to brave the Natchez Trace in a walk back to Kentucky from New Orleans. Merchants had a reasonable expectation that their goods would safely reach their destination, provided the water was high enough, but not too high. The steamboat was so much better than the flatboat. There was a honeymoon between the steamer and the natural Kentucky River, but like many honeymoons, it was short-lived.

During the honeymoon the first regularly scheduled runs were conceived: ads began to appear in the papers of the towns accessible to the river like Frankfort and Louisville touting regular service (during high water) to other river cities and stops in between. A typical 1831 Frankfort ad reads:[23]

> *The steamers, Sylph and Volant, are now in complete order, and have commenced business between Frankfort and Louisville (for which trade they were specially constructed), and will leave each port every other day.*

There were some "packet" boats on the water that carried only passengers, but most carried both freight on the main (or lower) deck and passengers on the upper decks with the pilot house (called the "Texas") on the top deck. The terminus points were between the major cities, but passengers and cargo were picked up at the numerous "landings" along the river. The landings were the small communities along the river, such as Gratz, Valley View, and Oregon or a farm landing where the land of a major farm that had both passengers and cargo touched the river and a boat could pull in to it. The Kentucky River steamers were small compared to the ones plying the Ohio and Mississippi with most of the runs connecting Frankfort with Louisville and Cincinnati, both of which could be reached in a single day. Most passengers and freight going on to ports farther up or downstream such as St. Louis, New Orleans or Pittsburgh would generally transfer to larger vessels at Louisville or Cincinnati for this journey. Few Kentucky River boats had overnight accommodations, but as time went on, the passen-

PACKETS ON THE RIVER

From the dawn of steam in about 1820 until viable traffic vanished from the river in about 1920 several hundred packet boats plied the Kentucky River. A true packet boat carried both freight (generally on the lower deck) and passengers (generally on the upper decks). Later excursion packets carried only passengers with the lower deck fitted for passenger use. The small "packet" was used for smaller excursions. The only remaining "packet" is the Dixie Belle *operating from the Shaker Landing in Pool 7. It conducts regular cruises in the summer with an annual special guided cruise each year with the Corps of Engineers' River Historian.*

Where the Ohio and Kentucky Waters meet, at Carrollton, Ky.

Cyde Bunch

Louisville District, U.S. Corps of Engineers

Louisville District, U.S. Corps of Engineers

gers expected more luxury in their daytime or deck accommodations, as noted from the ads of the time. In 1820, however, the steamer *Providence* advertised that it would pick up passengers and freight at Leestown (Frankfort) for passage to New Orleans. This was not the usual technique, however, as the larger steamers could much better accommodate overnight travel in terms of both room and board.

Kentucky River steamers varied in size from about 50 tons to a maximum of just over 200 tons. Outbound freight generally consisted of agriculture products like tobacco and goods of rough manufacture like hemp rope, bagging, or yarn. Upstream freight was luxury goods not made in Kentucky, such as glassware, fine cloth, and coffee as well as other necessities of life like farm tools and books. Shippers were often loyal to certain "Masters" or captains and would ship their goods only on boats under their control. Downstream (Frankfort to Louisville) freight rates were cheaper than upstream rates for the same distance, about $0.15 per 100 pounds downstream compared to about $0.25 per 100 pounds upstream.

The major enemies to shippers during this period were water conditions, snags, and explosions. The drafts required by the steamers were a major factor in their design, and under no circumstances could the steamer draft exceed five feet and expect to operate much of the year. The smaller craft, say about 50 to 75 tons, drew only about 2' and could ascend farther upriver than their larger sisters. All of the advertisements of regular schedules had disclaimers that service would continue "as long as the water will serve" or ". . . when the river was in good boating order." No one expected the boats to float on a trickle, nor could they buck a strong current during a flood.

Very modest efforts were made by the state legislature to clear the river of snags, but the papers contained frequent examples of boat sinkings due to a collision with a submerged log, tree, or rock. These accidents were more or less accepted as their frequency was far less than in the days of flatboats and keelboats. Boiler explosions were likewise accepted as part of the occupational risk, as within the living

LANDINGS

During the golden age of steam travel, there were over 100 "landings" along the Kentucky River from Carrollton to Beattyville. About two-thirds of these were located between Frankfort and Carrollton because this was the first area to have year round slackwater. Many were simple landings, like this, while some were substantial centers of commerce like Mundy's Landing.

Louisville District, U.S. Corps of Engineers

Kentucky Historical Society

memory of many persons of this period the Indians had poised a far greater threat to their lives than boilers ever would.

Frankfort and the River

Compared to Cincinnati on the Ohio River or St. Louis on the Mississippi, Frankfort on the Kentucky River may be in a different class, but their respective histories are as much intertwined as that of their much bigger sisters. Frankfort exists where it is and what it is because of the river, and the story of the river centers at Frankfort.

Their affair begins in 1751 when Christopher Gist, in the employ of the Ohio Land Company of Virginia, was seeking desirable lands for settlement west of the Allegheny Mountains. The farming practice on the tidewater plantations was to squeeze the most possible production out of land for a few years, generally tobacco, then move on to other land when the yield became low. This was generally in about two to three years. No fertilization, even animal waste, was used to replenish the land; hence, it was soon exhausted. Plantations of several thousand acres were thereby required to profitability cultivate a few hundred acres of land. Large quantities of cheap land were in demand by Virginia planters and a virtually inexhaustible supply of this lay beyond the mountains, still in Virginia.

Gist was sent out to find land that was suitable for eastern type farming, to survey it, and to claim it for the Ohio Land Company investors. Gist explored a large part of what is now Ohio, crossed the Ohio River, and made his way southward by following buffalo trails to the Kentucky River. He found a shallow spot on this river (near the mouth of Benson Creek), crossed it, and camped on some flat, marshy land that would one day be Frankfort. The shallow crossing and the flat land are two of the major reasons that Frankfort exists where it does, and there is a third reason: this point was on a major waterway from which bulky farm goods could be shipped downstream to world markets. Water transportation was the only way bulky goods could be moved in the 18th century, and this fact had to be in the mind of Explorer Gist.

Little came as a direct result of the Gist explorations, but during the early 1770's hardy settlers and surveyors began to trickle across the mountains into the wilds of Kentucky. Kentucky was, of course, still part of the crown colony of Virginia and subject to the laws of Virginia and the British Crown. The British Crown, acting through the colonial governors, could award large tracts of land, generally bounded by rivers and mountains, to whomever it pleased, but before individual parcels could be sold and claimed for settlement, proper ownership had to be established. Surveying and marking off specific parcels was the first order of business of land companies that intended to sell the land they had obtained from the Crown by grants.

Land parcels in most states are defined according to their position in specific, well-defined, land sections. These land sections are generally a surveyed checkerboard land pattern with absolute monuments set where four sections meet. Individual parcels are therefore defined according to their relationship to these monuments. In Kentucky, however, the surveyors did not wait for any absolute land pattern to be established upon which to define their parcel surveys but instead surveyed individual parcels within very large tracts of land which may or may not have ever been surveyed. The corners of a parcel were defined by physical objects (a tree, a large rock, the foot of a hill, a stream, or the like), and parcels were subject to extensive overlapping or gaps. Early Kentucky (or Virginia) had no tax maps upon which to record land ownership, but certain "proof" of ownership was sometimes used to assert claims in the event of later disputes. In the case of very early Frankfort, this proof of ownership by the McAfee Company in 1773 was a buried tomahawk and fish gig near a marked gum sapling.[24] These items were recorded in the deed books and could be recovered, if needed, to establish claim of ownership.

The earliest settlement near Frankfort was initiated by Captain Hancock Lee in 1775 as he came up the Kentucky River to the shallow buffalo crossing, earlier used by Gist. Lee was employed by the Ohio Land Company of Virginia to carve up a 200,000-acre land grant into 400-acre tracts, of which a site near present-day

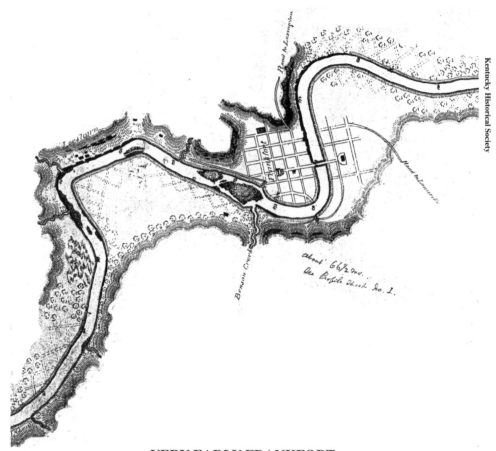

VERY EARLY FRANKFORT

This map, prepared in 1828 by the Corps of Engineers, shows why Frankfort is where it is. The sand bar created by Benson Creek created a shallow point in the river which could be forded much of the year. This was one of the major crossing points of the Kentucky River and was extensively used by early pioneers making their way to new lands west of the river. A settlement, ultimately Frankfort, grew up around this crossing point. Most of the streets shown in this map were the city laid out by General James Wilkinson on the land he owned in the 1780's.

Frankfort was one he called Leestown. This site was attractive because it had good springs, flat land, and a shallow river crossing.

Rude cabins began to rise at Leestown, and by 1780 and it became an assembly point of sorts for river travelers. In March of that year, Stephen Frank and others from the Lexington area were on their way to the salt springs of Bullitt's Lick (in present-day southern Jefferson County) to make salt for their settlements. They pulled out of the river at the shallows just upstream from Leestown to camp for the night. As they lay sleeping, a band of roving Indians in canoes attacked their campsite, killing Stephen Frank and wounding others. Word of the attack quickly spread to the settlements around the Bluegrass, and soon the river shallows upstream from Leestown were referred to as "Frank's Ford" later corrupted to "Frankfort".

The anchor that secured Frankfort (and Leestown) to the Kentucky River was set by General James Wilkinson. He came to Kentucky in 1783 with something less than an unblemished Revolutionary War record, but he had a highborn wife, important connections, a charismatic personality, boundless energy, a quick wit, and was totally without scruples. Virtually single-handed, he opened the port of New Orleans to Kentucky produce, much of which was to be placed on the Kentucky River at Frankfort. This port had been closed to goods from the United States by the Spanish authorities but Wilkinson, using every ounce of his important connections, charismatic personality, boundless energy, quick wit, and complete lack of scruples, opened it to Kentucky bourbon, tobacco, pork, beef, and other agricultural products. Until the coming of the railroads some seventy years later, much of the Bluegrass produce bound for world markets was loaded on the river at Frankfort and manufactured goods from around the world were unloaded there. Frankfort's place as the *Port of the Bluegrass* was secure.

Wilkinson's impact upon Frankfort, and indeed upon Kentucky as a whole, is immense. He could see better than anyone else the potential of a river port in the heart of the burgeoning wilderness, a land that had agricultural goods to ship to the world, but needed the manufactured products from the industrial world. He could plainly see the two-way river traffic as water was the only mode of transportation for 18th century goods. Wilkinson put his money where his mind was: he purchased much of what is now downtown Frankfort, laid out a town, built his own house there, set up a ferry, organized the local government, initiated public improvements like drainage ditches, and continued his efforts to ship goods to the Port of New Orleans. While much of this was self-serving, his impact was permanent and shaped Frankfort into what it was soon to become: the state capital.

The shallow ford where Frank had been killed was one of the few easy crossing points over the Kentucky River for early settlers making their way west. The roads of the bluegrass led to this point, making this a natural point of commerce and development, but many of the early settlers, if we can call them that, were river roustabouts who guided the clumsy flatboats to New Orleans and poled the keelboats upriver. But when it came time to select a capital for the new state, Frankfort's position on the river was a key factor in her selection. Until the advent of railroads in the late 1800's, Frankfort retained her dual personality as a river port and capital city.

Frankfort is the only city on the Kentucky River to grow on both sides of it. Wilkinson's original settlement was on the right side (descending) of the river with streets named by him (Wilkinson Blvd, Wapping Street, Miro Street, etc.), but the city soon spilled over to the other side, where the present capitol building now is. With Frankfort on both sides of the river, ferries became highly important to the daily life of the growing city, and several were chartered. One of the early acts of the Legislature, after Kentucky became a state with Frankfort as its capital, was to provide free ferry service to the citizens living on the south side of the river on election and court days. These legislators wanted the south side citizens to know from whence their help came.

Belle Pointe, across the river near Benson Creek, grew up as a separate town with its own mayor and council. Much later it was incorporated into Frankfort.

One of the principal sources of firewood for early Frankfort was the driftwood that accumulated on Fish Trap Island, a sand bar in the middle of the river created by Benson Creek. The sand bar could be approached during the summer when the water was low and the wood dry via the shallow ford which was at the end of this island. There was more wood here than the residents could use, or at any rate care to remove, and it became a hazard to the navigation that was developing. In 1803 Martin Hawkins was authorized to remove the wood with the payment for these services being the right to construct a low dam across the river and use the head created thereby to power a mill. The dam also contained a chute behind which descending boats could assemble. When certain planks behind the chute were removed, the rushing waters through the chute would carry the boats downstream, past the shallows. This arrangement worked quite well for descending traffic, but was a barrier to upstream traffic and was ordered removed after less than one year's operation. The plans for this dam and mill have long since vanished, if they ever existed, but Mr. Hawkins certainly deserves credit as one of the early entrepreneurs, engineers, and lockmasters on the Kentucky River. There have been many to follow.

Like all river towns, Frankfort was subject to the whims of the river around which it was built. The Kentucky River at Frankfort has recent measured flood peaks of more than 40' above normal flow elevation. The flood waters would totally surround many of the houses and buildings and would carry lighter, outbuildings with them, leaving behind water filled cellars and stagnant ponds in the low-lying areas. The citizens had no hope of any flood control works, but did construct drainage ditches and sewers to carry away water left by the receding floods.

Crossing the river at a shallow ford or on ferries was no more convenient to early 19th-century citizens than it is today. They wanted bridges. There was business to be conducted on both sides of the river. Bridging a river with a 40' flood rise is a major undertaking with 20-21st century technology and was nearly beyond the power of frontier Kentucky engineering. A pontoon bridge was constructed between Ann Street (north side) and Shelby Street (south side) in 1806 and a second pontoon bridge following later at the foot of Wilkinson Blvd. These pontoons were flatboats, anchored to the river bottom with planking across them to carry carriages. It is not known how river traffic got by floating bridges, but the bridge probably contained one movable pontoon that could be loosened to permit the passage of river traffic then reinstalled. How they handled high water is likewise obscure, but they likely took the whole bridge loose during high water. Pontoon bridges have many drawbacks, but they are better than ferries or shallow fords.

Frankfort had business to conduct on both sides of the river in all weather and continued to cry for a permanent, all-weather bridge. In 1810 the Legislature established the Frankfort Bridge Company to erect such a bridge at a cost not to exceed $30,000. Shares of $100 each were issued and tolls charged to repay the shareholders. It was also stipulated that the bridge be not less than 60' from its foundation (to permit river traffic during high water) and that not more than one pier be in the river channel. This was neither the first nor last time politicians dictated the specifications of a bridge, to their ultimate sorrow.

This bridge was a wooden bridge, typical of the day, with an abutment on each bank and the single pier in the center. It served well until the icy winter of 1832 hurled large chunks of ice against the center pier. The ice, combined with a massive buildup of driftwood against the center pier, weakened the entire structure so that traffic was halted across the bridge and ferries were once again put into service. Repair work was undertaken on the bridge in 1833, but as the work was nearing completion, the entire midsection fell into the river.

A Connecticut contractor with his own patented bridge design was retained in 1834 to rebuild the bridge. His bridge was completed, and the integrity of its strength was tested on November 29 by driving fat bullocks over it. (It is noted that the most recent bridge over the Kentucky River at Frankfort, built in the 1980's, was tested by parking loaded trucks on it.) Unfortunately, this bridge also fell into the river on Christmas Eve 1834, with some loss of life. Frankfort commuters still had to cool their heels on the unreliable ferries for more than a decade.

Engineers have a knack for bad timing: they build a pipeline down the middle of a street after it has been repaved or close a street for repairs during the rush hour. In Frankfort, the next bridge was built after Lock #4 created a 20' deep pool behind it. Extensive cofferdams were now needed to build bridge piers where modest cofferdams would have served prior to the lock construction. Nevertheless, a completely new bridge was built at the St. Clair Street site some four years after Lock #4 was placed in operation. This bridge was a toll bridge, had a stone pier, and was covered. Construction began in 1844, was completed in 1847, and it continued in service until 1896 when it was replaced by the present "singing bridge". North and south Frankfort were now securely and permanently tied together.

Because it was the center of Bluegrass commerce, boatbuilding rapidly became a major industry in early Frankfort. The original boats were, of course, flatboats designed and built for the one-way trip to New Orleans. These were built to order, with two weeks being a maximum time for construction of a flat boat about 14'x45'. No records exist of the number of these built in Frankfort, but more were built there than any other one place on the river.

The advent of steam changed everything. After the early steamers began to ply western waters, flatboats continued to be a cheap way to haul bulky goods to downstream ports, mainly New Orleans and Natchez, but steamers began to nudge them out of the water. The earliest recorded steamer built in Frankfort was in 1810, but little is known of it. In 1818 the Frankfort firm of Hanson and Boswell built a steamer of 80 tons burden for the Frankfort-Louisville trade (during high water, of course). The construction of other steamers followed.

Source: Kentucky Historical Society

19TH CENTURY FRANKFORT

The picture above shows how the river surrounds Frankfort on three sides. The bridge on the right is the 1847 covered bridge at the site of the present-day singing bridge on St. Clair Street. The toll house to this bridge can be seen at the left end of the bridge. The bridge on the left is the 1851 RR bridge. Wilkinson Boulevard is the major street on left-center.

The picture below appears to have been taken when the St. Clair Street bridge was new and the toll house was under construction, as seen at the left end of the bridge. The courthouse was the dominant feature in this picture.

The construction of the lock/dam system from the mouth of the Ohio River to Frankfort in 1842 changed more in Frankfort than the advent of steam: commerce and people could now move on the river all year instead of just during high water and Frankfort was the end of the line for both steamers and rail. People and freight moved from rail to steam and visa versa. During the early 1840's as many as thirty different boats made daily trips between Frankfort and the downstream river cities of Louisville and Cincinnati, hauling both passengers and freight. The early 1840's was the true golden age of river travel to and from Frankfort. It was fast, safe, comfortable, reliable, and cheap for both passengers and freight. The land roads were none of these. In the late 1840's and early 1850's, however, when the railroads went on to Louisville and the maintenance of the locks became almost nil, major river traffic from Frankfort took a nose-dive and never looked up again.

Beginning with the advent of steam, Frankfort was a major "sawmill town". In the early days of steam these iron monsters were totally static, that is, they stayed in one place all their life because they were simply too heavy and bulky to move anywhere. The timber from the headwater area was floated downstream to the mills at Frankfort (and other places) for sawing into lumber. At first, individual logs were "branded" by the farmer who cut the tree and floated it downstream. Losses from this technique were very high, and by the 1830's logs were bound together with grapevine into rafts about 10' to 16' wide and 100' to 150' long. The rafts were manned by three to five hands and were stopped by log booms (heavy chains) across the river. Generally, specific rafts were headed for specific mills, the owner of which had made prior arrangements for the shipment of logs. He would pull the raft from the water, cut the logs into lumber, and ship it from Frankfort by rail or steamer. Following the winter and spring "tides," when the logs could be floated down from the small headwater streams where they were cut, there would often be several miles of rafts waiting removal and sawing at Frankfort.

When steam-driven mills became lighter and more mobile, they were built in the headwater towns (Jackson, Beattyville, etc.), much nearer the source of their cutting. This, together with the rail lines that were reaching these communities, made it more economical to saw the logs in these towns and place the cut lumber on rail there. Major sawmills in Frankfort faded into history.

By far the most lasting effect that the river had upon Frankfort was the Corps of Engineers' headquarters for the Kentucky River lock and dam system located there. It was the nerve center for the entire system with heavy-duty shops, maintenance personnel, work boats, and supervisory personnel located at Lock #4, just downstream from Frankfort. Over two-dozen full-time labors, boat hands, and supervisors plus seasonal labor were located there. The shops had foundries, machine shops, and all the needed equipment to keep the locks and work boats working. The lockmasters at lock #4 were provided with better-than-adequate housing, with the other labors coming from the town's work force. When the Corps of Engineers pulled out of Frankfort, it was a major loss to the economy of the city, as well as to the maintenance of the locks.

To Frankfort of the 21st century, the Kentucky River is more of a problem than an asset since it floods. The Corps of Engineers has protected much of the city from flooding with flood walls, but many buildings, some in the historical district, still get their basements filled during a good high-water. Wet basements notwithstanding, Frankfort is where it is and what it is because of the Kentucky River. Settlers headed west no longer cross at the shallows near Benson Creek, the house built by General James Wilkinson is no more, riverboats no longer lower their gangplanks on St. Clair Street, nor are rafts of logs pulled from the water for sawing, but the capital city of Kentucky has an eternal debt to the river that winds through it.

The Kentucky River and Kentucky Counties

When the new world was "owned" by Europeans, vast expanses of land were granted to favored companies or individuals by the monarch who claimed such ownership. These monarchs had no idea of what they were granting, but the expanses were defined by nebulous rivers and mountain ranges. When independence was won by the colonies in the late 1770's, the unsettled land granted by the British monarchs came with the colonies, and it was up to the colony with the best claim to the prior grant to establish its jurisdiction over the unsettled areas. Kentucky fell into this category.

Virginia had the best claim to most of what is now Kentucky, with New York claiming part of it. New York did not abandoned its claim until 1782, but in reality Kentucky (except for the Jackson Purchase area in western Kentucky) was part of Virginia's Fincastle County. This was a large county that extended on both sides of the Appalachian Mountains and meant that all official county business had to be conducted east of this barrier.

It is the Anglo-Saxon mindset that larger areas, like a country or a state, be sub-divided into smaller areas, like a county, for the purpose of local government, local records, local commerce, and sometimes spiced with a pinch of local graft and corruption. In 1776 a petition was set before the Virginia legislature to make Kentucky a separate county, which was granted. Except for the Jackson Purchase, Kentucky County, Virginia, was essentially modern Kentucky. Even with this concession, Kentucky County was ungovernable and had to be further subdivided. This is where the Kentucky River comes in.

Immediately after the Revolutionary War, there were a few settlements in Kentucky, but no real maps and no fixed (or absolute) survey points from which to define land boundaries. Everything of importance had to be defined by physical features, and rivers fit this concept very nicely. The 1778 and 1781 Virginia legislatures had set aside land around the Green River as a reward to Revolutionary War soldiers for their services, but much of the prime Kentucky River land had been granted to French and Indian War veterans. Most of this was not claimed or occupied until after the Revolutionary War.

In 1780, while Kentucky was part of Virginia, Kentucky County was divided into three local units, for which the Kentucky River was the major dividing line. These counties were: Fayette County, which was bounded on the west and south by the Kentucky River, on the north by the Ohio River and on the east by a nebulous line through the mountains; Jefferson County, which was bounded on the east by the Kentucky and Dick's (Dix) Rivers, on the north by the Ohio River, and on the west and south by a hazy line more or less the Green and Cumberland Rivers to the present Tennessee line; and Lincoln County, which was bounded on the north by the Kentucky River, on the east by a hazy north-south line near present-day Harlan County, on the south by the Tennessee line, and on the west by Jefferson County, wherever that might be. The Kentucky River was the only true dividing line between these counties, and this appears on the classic 1784 Filson Map of Kentucky. The Kentucky River was a natural county boundary as it was almost impossible to cross during about half of the year and thereby formed a natural barrier to routine county business affairs. Kentucky settlers were happy to go to their county seats without having to cross this river.

While still under Virginia's thumb, additional counties were created which were bounded by the Kentucky River: Mercer County, bounded on the east by the Kentucky River, was carved from Jefferson County; Bourbon County, bounded on the south by the Kentucky River, and Woodford County, bounded on the west by the Kentucky River, were carved from Fayette County; and Madison County, bounded on the north by the Kentucky River, was carved from Lincoln County. At this point (1785-9) no county line crossed the Kentucky River due mainly to getting across it during much of the year. By Kentucky standards, these counties were very large, but the settlements were very few and far apart. Candidate towns for county seats were in short supply.

After Kentucky gained its independence from Virginia (1792), more settlers continued to pour into the new state, and the need for county seats closer to the people increased, new counties along the Kentucky River were carved from the larger ones: Clark (1792), Franklin (1794), Garrard (1796), Gallatin (1798), Henry (1798), Jessamine (1798), Estill (1808), and Clay (1807). Of these new and existing downstream counties (that is below the three-forks), only Franklin, Gallatin, and Estill had boundaries that crossed the river. All the others had boundaries that went with the river but did not cross it, meaning that all of the county and the county seat were on the same side of the river. The principal reason that Franklin County spanned the river was the shallow ford near Benson Creek making it easy to get from one side to the other during low water and the fact that Frankfort was growing up on both sides of the river. There was no other town on the downstream river that grew up this way.

Owen County (1819) and Anderson County (1827) were carved from other counties with borders that ran with the river, but no other downstream county was created that crossed the river.

Above the three-forks, however, all of the county lines cross the river, for it is the only artery into this region and all of the settlement in the area is along both of its banks. Above the three-forks, the river was fordable much of the year and was not a major barrier to travel. The natural barriers in eastern Kentucky are the mountain ridges, and they form most of the county lines with the Kentucky River running through their middle.

The Twilight of the Flatboat

The flatboat trade all the way to the lower Mississippi did not die out as soon as the steamers hit the water; in fact, it prospered more than before steam. Flatboats were the "low tech" carrier of the day and could still be owned and operated with little capital; a sinking meant the loss of cargo only if a flatboat was worth less than $200. They could ply waters not accessible to even the lowest draft steamer and could be put in just about anywhere. Most importantly, however, the crews that took them to the lower Mississippi could now return home in relative safety and convenience aboard a steamer. Some served as crew, mainly by carrying wood onto the vessel, and some were merely deck passengers, but in either case, they had a good chance of getting home in good health. Deck passage fare dropped from ten to three dollars between 1825 and 1855, not including food, which meant that a Kentucky boatman would get home with most of his $50 pay.

The major impact of this aspect of the steam age was that flatboatmen could now be family men, a luxury not available to them when they had to walk back home from Louisiana.

The flatboat could not, however, long survive the competetion of the steamer. By the 1840's steamer service had taken over on the lower Kentucky River, but barges of heavy cargo from the three-forks area continued their one-way journey to the Lexington and Frankfort markets during high water.

The Push for Slackwater

Frankfort was by far the most active downstream port, but brave owners and masters knew of the vast, unserved freight and passengers upstream of Frankfort. The following ad appeared in the April 6, 1841 *Frankfort Commonwealth:*[25]

For Boonsborough, Ky. River

The splendid steamer OCEAN, J. T. Brooks, master, will leave for the above and intermediate ports on Friday, the 9th April at 1 o'clock, P.M.
For freight or passenger apply on board, or to
C. BASHAM, Jr.

N.B. Should the water be too low at that time in the Kentucky river, the Ocean will positively make the trip the first rise of the water thereafter.

April 6, 1841

About half a century would pass before anything resembling regular schedules much above Frankfort would come to pass.

The ears of the legislature in Frankfort were not dull during the 1830's. As steam vessels became more dependable and comfortable and the economy was emerging from raw frontier towns to Bluegrass centers of commerce and learning, the cry for dependable transport beyond Kentucky borders was heard. The conception of the next life had taken place.

CORPS OF ENGINEERS WORKBOAT KENTUCKY GOING DOWNSTREAM THROUGH LOCK 9 AT VALLEY VIEW.

The two imposing lockmaster houses are gone now, but the small office between them is still in use as an office. The RINEY-B Railroad with its trestle over Marble Creek is in the background.

Note the timber barge-guidewalls at the ends of the lock chamber.

Life Three

THE GOLDEN AGE
OF THE LOCKS AND DAMS
(1842-1932)

Slackwater Dream

The passenger packet service to Louisville, Cincinnati, and river points beyond that began in 1816 gave the Bluegrass nobility, as well as the common folk, a taste of travel in relative comfort, economy, and speed. Steamboat travel was a dream come true as the wealthy traveler could reach his destination in complete comfort and relative safety, while the average person on the deck below could stand at the rail, enjoy the passing scenery, and leisurely dine on the provisions with which he had provided himself for the journey. But rich or poor, they wanted to be able to travel all the time, not just when the Kentucky River was at the right stage.

In addition, the flatboat trade to the lower Mississippi continued to thrive. This was still a relatively cheap way to get large quantities of bulky goods downstream if there were no intention of a return trip. But the merchants who used flatboats or steamers wanted to sell goods year round, and the deckhands who guided these comfortless cubes downriver during the winter storms and ice wanted to also be able to travel in the relative comfort of summer and fall when the river was often too low to float them.

The concept of slackwater all the way into the three-forks area dominated the early 19th-century commercial mind. The difficulty of moving the natural resources of the three-forks area together with the agricultural produce of the Bluegrass to the downstream markets was totally overwhelming as the hazards of the natural river were great and the time the river could be used was limited. Merchants and farmers alike felt strangled, even after steamboats offered some degree of two-way travel for part of the year. Railroads were beginning to be built in populated areas of the eastern seaboard, but were nowhere near the Kentucky border. They were not a factor in moving early 19th-century freight in large quantities. Slackwater was the only way to do this. Had a giant hand dropped locks and dams on the Kentucky River from its mouth to the three-forks area in 1820 when salt, iron, coal, and timber were waiting to move to downstream markets, the history of eastern Kentucky might have been different from what it is. But no such hand appeared, and the three-forks resources and Bluegrass produce had to wait for the spring "tides" to move.

Improvements to the river to this point had been limited to the clearing of snags, sandbars and the rocks. This helped the steamboats during high water, but was by no means the complete answer. Only slackwater was the answer of the upstream holders of minerals and timber rights.

Mustering what political pull they had in Washington, the Kentucky delegation in 1828 convinced Congress to initiate a Federal survey of the Kentucky River. Lieutenants William Turnbull and Napoleon B. Buford of the Army Engineers were assigned the task of developing a plan for the improvement of navigation as far as possible upriver. This survey was completed to Boonesboro, the site of Daniel Boone's original fort, within the year with the recommendation that an experimental dam be built near Frankfort for the purpose of:[1]

> *"...... the determination of the practicability and expediency of the construction of navigation improvements on the Kentucky and similar inland rivers.*

The estimated cost of this dam was $10,704. Primarily because the Kentucky River lies entirely within one state, the Federal government declined to fund the project, and the Federal involvement on the Kentucky River was postponed for 50 years.

The need for navigation improvement did not die with the Federal withdrawal from the concept. The agricultural products of the Bluegrass as well as upriver goods, such as salt, iron products, timber, and coal had ready, year-round markets downstream. The Kentucky legislature responded to this need, and in 1835 commissioned Major R. Philip Baker, who had worked on the Tennessee River and a canal in Alabama, as State Engineer specifically to examine the techniques to improve the navigation on the Kentucky River at least to the three-forks area near Beattyville where much of the coal and timber centered.

The First Five Locks/dams

Major Baker determined, in 1835, that year-round navigation could be attained to this point by the construction of fifteen locks and dams on the river with a dry weather draft of six feet, ample to float steamboats and flatboats of that day. Each lock would raise (or lower) a boat about 14' to 15' to create a constant pool the entire 255 miles with a rise in elevation of about 228'. The lock chambers Major Baker recommended were sized for the largest steamers of the day at 38' wide and 170' long rated at 250 tons. Since flatboats were built to make a one-way trip, they could easily be built to conform to the lock dimensions and were not a factor in the lock chamber sizing. The State was to provide the capital for the project and collect tolls to pay off the bonds sold to build the structures.

A summary of Major Baker's 1835-38 very comprehensive survey is as follows:[2]

Improvement	Miles of Stream	Cost
17 Locks/dams on main stem	250	$1,950,868
Lockmaster houses and other main stem items		150,298
North Fork locks/dams	55	502,700
Middle Fork Improvement Fork	68	750,000
16 Locks/dams on South Fork	42	1,099,746

In his report to the Legislature, Major Baker observed that the tolls might not be adequate to pay the entire cost of the project to the three-forks area, but argued for their construction:[3]

> *In the present condition, even with the most favorable tide, the river affords but a precarious and hazardous navigation, and in consequence, nearly the whole of the transportation required by this extensive district of country is driven to the expensive and tardy resort of road wagonage. Hence, many articles, and the natural resources of the country, and such as would be produced if easy and cheap communications were offered for their carriage, are either entirely neglected or are produced to a very limited extent. This is especially true in relation to the various resources presented by the mines and forests of the mountain districts which are of the first necessity to the inhabitants of the older settled parts of the State, but which will not bear the cost of land transportation.*

Major Baker was not a man of small thought and continued his survey to a connecting link between the South Fork and the Cumberland River. This project would require a lift of about 160' up to the elevation of the Cumberland River, a canal about 38 miles long, reservoirs to store water for the canal during the dry season, and a tunnel about 700 to 800 yards long near Cumberland Gap. The Major did not make a cost estimate of this component of the project, but it was reexamined in 1872 by the Corps of Engineers and priced at $818,000. Prudently, nothing came of it.

Failures of dams similar to those proposed on the main stem of the Kentucky River were all too common in that day. The State, acting upon Major Baker's advice, retained the services of Silvester Welch, an experienced engineer who had supervised the successful construction of ten locks and dams on the Kiskiminetas River near Pittsburgh. Engineer Welch brought with him several other experienced assistant engineers including William B. Foster, brother of Stephen C. Foster, who had enjoyed, for a short period, his *Old Kentucky Home*.

Kentucky Historical Society

THE WERNWAG BRIDGE

The Wernwag Bridge crossed the Kentucky River where present-day US 27 (south of Nicholasville) now crosses. This bridge was an engineering marvel when it was built in 1838 at a cost of $30,000. During the Civil War it was a very heavily guarded point as it was on the main supply line from the Union-operated Camp Nelson immediately north of the bridge.

The bridge remained in service until 1926 when a leaky roof permitted the wooden floor to rot.

Two other bridges have been built here including the US 27 bridge which crosses high above this level. Parts of these stone embankments can still be seen at this site.

The location of this bridge is near the mouth of Hickman Creek which was a major crossing point and place of activity during the early settlement of Kentucky.

Feeling the sense of the tight-fisted Kentucky legislature, Mr. Welsh and his assistants downsized the lock chambers to 38' x 145', sufficient to pass a 200-ton steamboat, slightly lowered the lift of each lock so that seventeen would be required to sustain a pool to Beattyville, and estimated the total cost of the seventeen structures at $2.3 million.

The design of the dams was marginal even by the standards of that day, but totally unthinkable now: a stair-step of stone-filled timber cribbing. A checkerboard system of oak and poplar timber cribbing was spiked together and filled with rock to make up the dam and keep the timber from floating away. Sometimes other debris was placed in the cribbing structure, but it was anything but watertight. No concrete, even a cap, was used. The spillway was a series of steps of heavy white oak planks spiked to the timber cribbing as they projected from the dam, as giant steps, down which the water would cascade. To those who have witnessed the power of water as it goes over the present concrete spillways, it is easy to imagine the wear and tear of the water upon the spillway as it descended wooden plank steps. Silt was trapped behind the cribbing and between the rocks to form the water-holding component of the dam. Maintenance was very high as both floods and ice took out chunks of the rock and the spillway planking almost each year. Repair of the structures in the "wet" was not simple, but had to be done as there was no other way.

The lock chambers, however, were solid stone masonry, and the major parts of the original masonry are still in use.

Until the advent of the income tax in the 20th century most income to units of government was from "user fees" like tolls, tariffs, and from land taxes. To build the dams on the Kentucky River, bonds were sold and were expected to be paid back from the tolls collected from the river users like modern revenue bonds for toll roads. The general coffers of the Kentucky treasury, as well as those of most other trans-mountain states, were not well filled and could by no means bear the cost of these major improvements. But the coal/timber producing area around Beattyville, from whence most of the heavy commercial tonnage would originate, continued to bring pressure upon Frankfort for slackwater to the three-forks area. Engineer Welsh and the Board of Internal Improvement sensed this and so warned the legislature that the traffic generated downstream alone would not generate sufficient income to amortize the loan taken out to build the first five structures (estimated at $701,405). Sensitive to the voters who would benefit from lower river travel, the Legislature authorized the construction of the first five structures, which would place slackwater past Frankfort, but not as far as Lexington.

Construction of locks #1 through #5 took place between 1836 and 1842, but little went right from the outset of the process: there were few contractors with successful experience in dam building; the bids came in higher than expected; building materials and skilled labor were in short supply; the State was experiencing financial and credit difficulties; some of the contractors went bankrupt; and there were foundation problems at some of the sites selected for the dams, to name a few. The total expenditures for the first five structures was $901,932 compared to the original $700,000 estimate. Later claims by the contractors ran the total cost to about $1.1 million. To near-bankrupt Kentucky, this was totally out of line, and the three-forks area, for which the system was really built, was still 166 miles away. There were no plans to go any farther at that time.

The five original dams created a slackwater system 95 miles long, but only the lower 66 miles could be used for steamer traffic at high water due to the bridges in Frankfort. Keelboats could pass under these bridges year 'round, but steamers could get under them only at minimum pool stages. A surveying error also caused the miter sills to be misplaced reducing the 6' draft expected.

As predicted, the tolls collected from passenger and cargo lockage were barely adequate to maintain the system, with little left to repay the capital. Very complex and frequently-changed toll rates were set by the state legislature to balance the needs of the bondholders, river users and voters. The tolls for 1842-43 were set as follows:[4]

	Per Lock
Freight per ton, by boat, descending	10 cents
Freight per ton, by boat, ascending	15 cents
Cabin passengers	6 1/4 cents
Children, servants, and deck passengers	half fare
Livestock	3 1/2 cents
Household furniture, carriages and other shipment	5 % of transportation rate

The January 1852 rates were, in part:

	Per Mile
Ascending freight, per 100 pounds	1/2 mill.
Descending freight, per 100 pounds	1/2¢
Cabin passengers over 12 years	5¢
Children, servants, and deck hands	3¢
Beef, pork, lard, per barrel	2¢
Sacks of corn or wheat, (2 1/2 bushels)	1/2¢

Tobacco, per hogshead	
Lock 1	30 cents
Lock 2	15 cents
Lock 3	10 cents
Lock 4	6 cents
Lock 5	5 cents
Steamboats, lockage per lock	$ 2.00
Flatboats and keelboats, empty, per linear foot, per lock	3 cents

Since the system did not extend to the three-forks area, or even close to it, the high tonnage items originating there such as coal, iron, salt, and timber were not realized and the income was barely enough to pay the high operation and maintenance cost of the locks and dams. At the aforementioned rate, a person traveling from Frankfort to Louisville, some 66 miles on the Kentucky River, would be assessed $0.33 in tolls. One ton of freight would be assessed $0.66. Such low rates were excellent for keeping Kentucky legislators in office but were not favorable to navigation system bondholders. During the first 24 years of system operation, from 1843 to 1866, the gross receipts amounted to $472,620 and the cost of system operation and maintenance was $314,489 leaving a net revenue of $158,131 to retire the $900,000 bonds.

The actual tonnage was reasonably high, as the Ohio Railroad ended at Frankfort and the goods from this rail line were placed on steamboats for their ultimate destination of Ohio River and Lower Mississippi ports. The population also enjoyed comfortable, cheap, and dependable travel up and down this part of the Kentucky River, a pleasure unknown elsewhere. The rates were just set too low. During the pre-Civil War period, however, the ultimate fate of the Kentucky River navigation was beginning to be written. The writing said: railroads. When the railroad from Frankfort to Louisville was constructed in 1852, the income to the river system took a nose-dive. In an effort to recoup some of this traffic, the tolls on the river were reduced by the Legislature, this had little effect on increasing traffic, but did reduce the amount of funds available for maintenance of the dams. Much more was to be taken away later in the three-forks area by the railroads.

During the Civil War, the river served the Union armies in several ways, but the maintenance of the structures was virtually non-existent during and immediately after the war. To make this worse, the Union army placed 3' of timbers on top of the dams to make up for the loss of water during the dry season. This created turbulence on the downstream face of the dam, hence accelerating the destruction of the wooden-planking spillway.

The system was yet a vital commercial and passenger link to those persons having access to it and had significance to the overall economy of central Kentucky in excess of the dollar value of the tolls collected. The floods of 1873 all but destroyed the flimsy dams (but not the solid locks) and rendered them more of a hindrance to navigation than a help. Commerce, hence the collection of tolls, came to a halt. This was particularly unfortunate as the retirement of the bonds with which the system was financed were retired with the tolls collected. Court action resulted and the control of the river, such as it was, moved into the hands of the creditors.

In the late 1870's there was much smoke, but little fire, at the State and local level to restore at least the five-lock system that had been built. A stock company had been chartered in 1852 and another in 1865 to take over the system and extend it to the three forks area. These failed. Because both money and politics were involved, very little was actually accomplished, though the apparent activity was great. By 1876 the five dams were in complete shambles. The pools were filled with debris, the wood cribbing that held the rock in place was rotten and rock fill was scattered. They were more of a hindrance to river traffic than a help. Even during high water, steamers had difficulty in navigating around them.

The substantially built locks, however, stood.

The Peak of Steamers on the Kentucky River

The solid period of marriage between steamers and the Kentucky River took place during the short span following the completion of the first five dams in 1842 and prior to the completion of the railroad to Louisville in 1852. During this decade steamers were the only transportation available, they could run on schedule, low fares were regulated by the legislature, and the steamers were safe and comfortable. Sleeping accommodations were on many packets between Frankfort and Louisville with meals included in the fare. There were more than one hundred "landings" between Frankfort and the Ohio River where the packets would pull in, on call. Based on the advertisements of the day, competition was stiff as there were several competing lines. The master of each steamer was part of the advertisement as it was important to the public that they pick the master of their choice for their journey. Schedules were planned around this. The using public did not know, or care, that the system was bankrupt.

Passenger comfort was also emerging as a factor in the selection of the "right" vessel. One of the early luxury vessels of this decade was the *Sea Gull*. Upon her maiden voyage to Frankfort, the *Frankfort Commonwealth* spoke of her fine furniture and her thick, soft carpets, concluding: [5]

> *Her cabins in elegance and neatness are unsurpassed. Her state rooms with the ladies' cabin are large and airy, with very large and comfortable spring beds and genuine hair mattresses. In short, the* Sea Gull *is without fault from her bowsprit to her rudder.*

The *Blue Wing* was likewise billed as a luxury vessel, with a ladies cabin that included: *a large, roomy and handsome bedstead with a trundle underneath it.* The *Blue Wing* was not bashful about going as far upstream as possible, far beyond the influence of the upper dam (#5). The March 17, 1846 *Frankfort Commonwealth* reports in the "local interest" section:[6]

The steamer Blue Wing, Capt. H. I. Todd, during the late flood in the Kentucky river ascended the Kentucky river a considerable distance higher than any steamer ever did before, having gone within ten miles of Irvine, the seat of justice of Estill County.

The inhabitants along shore, we understand, were exceedingly delighted with the novelty of the scene and manifested their pleasure by many acts toward the Captain and crew. We hope the day is not far distant, when steamers will arrive and depart daily at the three-forks, where so much coal, iron, and other natural resources lie.

Unless the Kentucky River flooded daily, regular service to Irvine would have to wait fifty years from the time this story was published.

Snags of all types as well as high water continued to take their toll upon the steamers that plied these waters, but most passengers and crew were saved during these events.

Major spas were built at Drennon Springs (Henry County) and Graham Springs (Mercer County). Some of their major clientele were the families of wealthy southern planters who came to Kentucky to escape the summer heat of the deep south. They would make their way by land or water to Louisville, where they would take a packet to the landing nearest to their destination. They came together with children, relatives, and servants to spend the summer months on the cooler Kentucky River and enjoy a summer social season with their summer peers as well as Kentucky nobility.

Rebuilding and Extending the System

Public works are initiated by politicians and public servants. These individuals are responsive to the public needs and have the power to pay for public works, with tax money or revenues. In 1873, Nathaniel S. Shaler, state geologist, began to speak out for river improvements. His interest was in the industrial development of the lower river, and he was a director of hemp-carpet backing and twine plant that used the power of the head of lock #4 at Frankfort. Some of the underpinnings of this works can still be seen at this lock. Geologist Shaler spoke widely for the redevelopment of the river and emphasized the positive influence it would have upon the Commonwealth. His associate in geology, Thomas Turner of Richmond, was later elected to Congress, where he helped get through legislation funding for a new survey of the river as well as construction funds. Judge Lysander Hord of Frankfort, later known as the Father of Kentucky River navigation, campaigned to get public as well as legislative support for river improvements.

The net effort of these three public servants was to restore the control of the ruined locks and dams to the state, away from the creditors into whose hands they had fallen through bond default. This transfer made it possible to spend public funds on their restoration and extension to the three-forks area.

Under contract with the Sinking Fund of Kentucky and by order of the governor, then later under the Rivers and Harbors Act of 1878 which contained a $3,000 river survey appropriation, two new surveys and reports on the Kentucky River were made in 1877 and 1878 well into the three-forks area. This work was under the direction of then Colonel William E. Merrill of the Corps of Engineers and by Robert H. Fitzhugh, a former Confederate Captain who had established himself in Kentucky as a railroad engineer and surveyor. A summary of these reports sets forth the following improvements:[7]

> *Repair of the five old locks and dams plus*
> *the construction of 12 new dams to extend*
> *slackwater to the mouth of the Middle Fork* $1,074,402
>
> *Extend slackwater for 121 miles up the North*
> *Fork by 21 locks and dams* $ 1,386,000
>
> *Extend slackwater for 69 miles up the South*
> *Fork and Goose Creek by 14 locks and dams* $ 968,000
>
> *Extend slackwater for 68 miles up the Middle*
> *Fork by 13 locks and dams* $ 786,000

Some of the data used for the reports had been compiled by Major Welsh in his 1837 survey.

Commenting on the cost-benefit ratio of the project, Capt. Fitzhugh thought it:[8]

> . . . . *supererogatory to enter into a detailed exhibit of the probable business to be developed by the proposed improvement, and especially so when the acknowledged productiveness of the counties involved is manifestly equal to the demands of any investment necessary to its relief from commercial thralldom.*

In modern words, Capt. Fitzhugh said, "Don't bother me with the numbers, just do it!" The modern economy of "counties involved" today depends upon the pools he and his successors created, but not close to the way he referred to in these straightforward words.

The figures and findings set forth in Captain Fitzhugh's reports were highly optimistic by any standards, but fell upon deaf Kentucky ears who were anxious to move goods out of the three- forks area but not anxious to tax voters to pay for it. It is also interesting to note that the report emphasized the feasibility of the old plan of connecting the South Fork with the Cumberland River at an estimated cost of $818,000. In 1878, the Kentucky legislature rejected a spending bill for river improvements, but did authorize the use of convict labor for renovation, if the counties would provide the material. The counties did not bite this hook. Judge Hord reentered the river improvement campaign by appealing to the voters in Frankfort and Franklin County to approve a bond issue. All of this was defeated and improvement of the Kentucky River appeared dead in 1878.

The "Rivers and Harbors Act of 1879" is invoked today as the basis of extensive federal involvement in the development of inland waters of the United States. It was one of the most comprehensive public works acts ever passed by Congress and ranks with the Interstate Highways Act some 75 years later as one of the major items of legislation affecting transportation in the country. This Act gave the Federal government wide powers, authority, and responsibility over the inland waterways of the nation, including the Kentucky River, and stipulated that no tolls would be charged for the passage of vessels through the locks and dams built under the Act. Colonel Merrill forwarded Captain Fitzhugh's report to Congress in time to be considered under this Act. Judge Hord and Geologist Shaler rushed to Washington who, together with Congressman Turner who was already there, testified on behalf of the Kentucky River for the inclusion of $100,000 to begin the march of the Corps of Engineers to the three-forks. They were successful and the Corps today cites the 1879 Rivers and Harbors Act as its authority to be on the Kentucky River.

Since the existing five locks and dams were in complete disrepair and no funds available to fix them, Kentucky officialdom had no problem in complying with the Act and immediately began the process of the transfer of the ruined structures to the Federal Government. The reverse of this process is currently (2001) under way as the Federal government is transferring the ownership of the upper ten structures to the state.

During the latter part of 1879 and the beginning of 1880, the paperwork to formally transfer the decayed five-lock system from state to the federal government was under way and on March 22, 1880 Kentucky conveyed ownership of the ruins of the five locks/ dams and adjoining land to the federal government. During the transfer negotiations, two interesting points arose. Kentucky wanted to continue as a "concurrent" owner of the reconstructed locks and dams. The federal government would have none of this and the word "concurrent" was deleted from the transfer papers.

Also, the right of Geologist Shaler to continue to use lock #4 to power his hemp mill was granted for a fee of $180 per year.

Because the 1877 report was in place, work on the lower five structures could begin immediately after the passage of the 1879 bill. The work was under the nominal direction of Colonel Merrill, head of the Cincinnati Corps of Engineers, but more directly by Captain James W. Cuyler, sent by the Corps for the daily direction of the work.

Work on the Kentucky River dams can be done only during the low-water season, meaning summer and fall. Not wanting to miss the 1880 construction season by the preparation of plans and specifications for bidding, Captain Cuyler determined to do the work directly by the government forces under his direction.

The restoration of the lock/dam system past Frankfort cost far more than the Federal government had anticipated. It was hoped that the foundations of the existing structures could be built upon, with the tops of the old dams removed and replaced, but for all practical purposes, the dams had to be completely replaced, due to their shoddy initial construction, but the locks themselves needed relatively minor repair. Captain Cuyler increased Captain Fitzhugh's cost estimate of $84,802 to $100,000 for dams #1-#4, as that was the funds he had available plus $35,000 for the repair of dam #5. The timber cribbing underpinning had to be ripped apart by hand piece by piece, which was a very slow process.

Floods during the restoration period did little to help the progress of the work. Cofferdams or the temporary dams that keep a river workplace dry while work is under way, are seldom built high enough to keep high water out. They are built to keep the work place dry during the summer months when work is under way but are overtopped by high water. Dam #1 was "flanked" by the flood of 1881. The riprap, or large protective stone, had not been put in place on the abutment opposite the lock by the time the flood hit, and the flood waters washed the abutment out thereby bypassing or "flanking" the dam. Captain Cuyler rushed to the site, fired the resident engineer, and ordered a row of piling to be driven across the breach against which timbers and stone could be placed to divert the river back into its original channel. This cost an unexpected $60,000.

By 1882, navigation as far upstream as Frankfort was restored. Dam #5 was completed in 1886, giving a total of 95 miles of slackwater. The obstructing bridge at Frankfort was replaced with a higher one so steamers could use the system in all but flood conditions.

The design of the new dams was still rock fill-timber cribbing except that they were of a more substantial nature. The spillways were still heavy white-oak planking spiked to the timber cribbing in a stairstep fashion. The dams were made more or less water-tight by leaving the dirt cofferdams across the upstream back of the dam. The lock walls were in good condition, but the gates were replaced. The concrete guidewalls, which guide boats and barges into and out of the lock chambers, were placed atop timber cribbing. Annual maintenance was, however, still a major cost and engineering problem. The winter floods simply ripped apart the rock-filled timber cribbing structures each year, and major work had to be done to restore them the next spring and summer. The well-built masonry locks still stood well during the winter floods and ice.

Locks #1 through #5 were operating well, carrying both passengers and freight of all types. Within three months of operation, the project had served 25 steamboats, 52 flatboats, 30 barges, and 128 rafts of logs. This was the first operational system of locks built by the Federal government, and in setting up the funding for the project, Congress had overlooked one element of a lock system: operational costs. Lockmaster houses were in

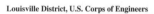

LOCK 4 BEFORE RECONSTRUCTION 1881

These photos show the deteriorated condition of lock 4 at Frankfort before its reconstruction in 1881. The original timber crib structure built in 1842 had simply given out due to a virtual total lack of maintenance and the very nature of timber crib construction. The hemp mill that paid $180 per year for the use of the head of this lock is seen in the background. The power wheel through which the water passed is in the vertical offset in the mill building. The foundation for this part of the structure can still be seen at Jim's Seafood. The screened intake to the power wheel is seen above..

DAM 4 RECONSTRUCTION, 1883

These photos show the reconstruction of Lock 4 at Frankfort. The original plans for this reconstruction in 1880 called for "repair" of the 1840 dam. When it was found that it was beyond repair, the old dam was completely torn apart, by hand, and rebuilt about 100' upstream from the old structure. Parts of the old dam can be seen in these photos. The reconstructed dam still used timber crib construction with no concrete used on the spillway. The logs were lifted by the steam powered derricks seen in these photos. The intake for the hemp mill had to be revised to accommodate the relocated dam position.

The lower-right photo is an excellent 1885 overview of the reconstruction of Dam 4 at Frankfort. The lock chamber is the original 1840 structure, but the dam, shown under construction, has been moved upstream (toward the top of the picture) from the 1840 dam because it was beyond repair. Note the timber barge guide walls extending from the lock walls. The hemp factory (present-day Jim's Seafood) is off the picture at left. The original timber-crib dam is being replaced with another timber-crib dam, as seen.

LOCK 1 FLANKED

While Lock 4 was under reconstruction in the fall of 1881, high water flanked, or washed around, the end of the dam as can be seen in these photos. The breach was repaired by driving two rows of wooden piles along the edge of the river and filling the space between the rows with dirt, trees and anything at hand to force the river back into its natural channel. Both photos show the double rows of wooden piling and the debris between them. The photo above (looking upstream) shows how the water flowed around the end of the dam then back into the channel. The stair-step timber crib dam is shown in the middle-left of the picture. The lock is out of the picture to the left. The photo below (looking downstream) shows the same double row of wooden piling with trees and other debris in the middle of them. The Corps of Engineers work-boat is in the background. The top of the timber crib dam is at right with the lock chamber off to he right of this photo.

place, but no funds had been set up to pay the lockmasters. Captain Cuyler asked for permission to charge tolls to pay the lockmasters, which was denied. He spent, and actually overspent, all of the construction funds he had to pay them; then he closed the locks in May 1882 and laid off the lockmasters. This made many Kentuckians very unhappy very quickly. The Corps of Engineers "found" some funds to pay the lockmasters and Congress ultimately created an "indefinite" appropriation as a standing fund for the operation of the locks and dams.

Like many engineers, Captain Cuyler was caught between bureaucratic/political tardiness and the desire of the public for instant gratification. Creditors, holding $6,000 in notes with which he had paid the lockmasters before the Federal government "found" some money to pay them, held a public meeting in Frankfort in August 1882 and resolved that he be "investigated." His closing of the locks in the previous May had precipitated the meeting and won him few friends on the river for which he had labored hard to develop. The investigation centered around the $325,000 set up by Congress for the repair of the first five dams, his choice of personnel, the schedule for restoration of traffic to Frankfort, and cost overruns. Suffering from intense nervous depression, he took leave of the Kentucky River and died on April 10, 1883. The dams built by Captain Cuyler are still standing, though in a modified condition.

Since this was one of the early forays of the Corps of Engineers into lock ownership and operation, uniform rules of staff discipline for all the locks operated by the Corps had not yet been established. The 1886 Annual Report of the Corps of Engineers states that Kentucky River lockmasters became a discipline problem, but this was put to rest by initiating uniform operating rules for all Corps operated locks.

Captain James C. Post, who was appointed to succeed Captain Cuyler, completed the work on dam #5 and began the planning on lock and dam #6, the first to be built by the Corps from the ground up. The system was functioning well, however, and both passengers and cargo were enjoying the fruits of Captain Cuyler's labors. The enthusiasm of a local resident is attested in a 1886 Letter to the Editor of the (Harrodsburg?) Democrat. This letter was written by "WLJ" (gender unknown) concerning a trip from Oregon (KY, at the upper end of pool #5) to Frankfort, some 30 miles away, to see the Barnum Circus:[9]

> *When we arrived within four or five miles of Frankfort the attention of all on board was attracted to the vast number of rafts that lined the shore on either side, until only a narrow channel was left in the middle of the river for the passage of steamers. These rafts continue in an almost unbroken line from the point I have mentioned to Frankfort, containing unnumbered thousands of the finest logs that ever floated to market representing an item that is of commercial interest to the entire state if not, indeed, to the whole civilized world. If anyone has any doubt of the value of improvements on the Kentucky River, a single trip along the quiet stream will give him an ocular demonstration that will be of practical utility in dispelling his delusion.*

This letter also discusses the social activity that took place among the 275 passengers on board the steamer.

Louisville District, U.S. Corps of Engineers

REPAIR OF LOCK 5 IN 1883

Some of the foundations of Lock 5 could be salvaged for reconstruction and the dam was rebuilt on top of the 1842 foundation. This photo shows barge-loads of timbers (lower right) and barges of large rock to fill between the timbers being placed by the several steam-driven derricks in the photo. The wooden planking on the two lower spillway steps is beginning to be placed. The Corps of Engineers work-boat Grace Morris *is on the downstream side of the dam nudging a rock barge into place.*

If one were seeking the true high point of Kentucky River navigation, it would be the ten years following the operation of Lock #5 in 1885. Information from the Corps of shows the following sample of data for this period.[10]

Year	Total Tonnage	Number of Lockages
1885		3422
1890	323,215	
1893	330,449	6962
1895	296,318	6780
1898	121,277	

When the turn of the century arrived, the railroads had replaced the river as the heavy freight carrier of choice in the Kentucky River valley.

LOCK 4 WITH HEMP MILL

A good view of the hemp mill using the power of dam four to operate the plant.

The water intake is the concrete framework directly at the far end of the dam, some of which can still be seen from Jim's Seafood today. The power wheel is in the tall building just to the left of the dam.

Comparing this picture with the Dam 4 Pre-construction photos, it can be seen that the new dam was relocated considerably upstream from the original site. Modifications to the water intake were needed to accommodate the revised dam location.

The owner of the hemp mill paid $180 per year for this power, a bargain at any time.

The Beartrap of Beattyville

A novel entry into the annals of engineering is posted at this period: *the Beartrap of Beattyville*. The extensive shipments of coal and timber in the three-forks area had to await the event of "tides" or high water before they could move downstream. Prior to "tides," these goods piled up in the three-forks area without generating cash for their owners, who had already paid hard currency to move them to this point. Anything to get the goods moving was good news to them. The slackwater system was still 166 miles downstream. In 1882 Congress appropriated $75,000 for a *lock and movable dam at Beattyville*. These funds were set up without the benefit of engineering studies by the War Department. When subjected to engineering examination the plan was changed to a fixed dam with a movable barrier in front of the lock chute at a revised cost of $115,412. The "Beartrap of Beattyville" was the result of this endeavor. Construction took place in 1885 and 1886.

A "Beartrap" was a two-leaf wooden structure that was raised by the hydraulic upstream head and lowered by taking the upstream head away, suddenly. A beartrap ride was a rapid, one-way journey downstream through a 300 foot chute from the upper pool to the lower pool. Coal-filled barges and other commercial vessels would gather at the upper pool near the Beartrap to await the filling of the upper pool and the sudden release of the gates. Upon the release of the leaf structure, water would pour through the movable gate assembly, taking with it all the craft that could maneuver into the path of the fast-moving water for the ride downstream in the chute and hopefully to their destination atop this artificial "tide." Water would continue to pour through the chute as long as there was a head differential between the pools. When the water no longer passed through the chute, traffic was stopped, the valve to raise the movable dam was opened, and the upper pool refilled as the dam raised. Refilling the pool could take a few days, depending upon the flow in the river at that time.

The downstream ride proved to be more of a hazard to both craft and men than the engineers had counted on. The barges, built for one-way more-or-less slackwater conditions, took the choppy ride downstream very poorly, inducing many of the frightened deckhands to jump off the semi-guided water craft before a crash against the guidewalls occurred or a crash resulted from their sudden departure from the barge.

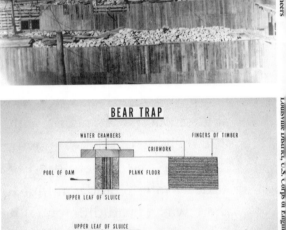

THE BEARTRAP
OF BEATTYVILLE

In the 1880's it was obvious that many years and dollars would be required to reach the coal fields of the Three-Forks area with slackwater. The Beartrap of Beattyville was an innovative, but unsuccessful, attempt to short circuit this problem. The idea was to create an artificial "tide" or crest of water to carry flatboats of coal from the Beattyville coal fields to the slackwater near Frankfort, some 100 miles downstream. This was to be used before the intermediate dams were built. The concept called for a low dam to be built across the river and the construction of two 300' long chutes through which the flatboats would begin their downstream ride. The drawing on the right shows the "beartrap" device, at the head of each chute, which could be raised hydraulically to create a pool of water behind them. The flatboats desiring to go downstream would gather in this pool near the upstream entrance of the chutes. When the beartrap was triggered (dropped) the pool of water would rush through the chutes, carrying the flatboats with them. This device was used only about one year then declared unsuccessful.

BEAR TRAP

WATER CHAMBERS
CRIBWORK
FINGERS OF TIMBER
POOL OF DAM
PLANK FLOOR
UPPER LEAF OF SLUICE

UPPER LEAF OF SLUICE
WATER LINE
CRIBWORK
FINGERS OF TIMBER
WATER LINE
WATER CHAMBERS

After about one year of operation, the "beartrap" technique proved that it was unsuitable for river navigation, and an effort was made to replace it with a conventional lock. In any event, the entire structure was demolished in 1891, and any usable equipment was shipped downstream where lock #6 was under construction. Railroads were nearing the three-forks area by 1890, thereby negating the economics of an isolated structure there.

March to the Three-Forks

The plans for the construction of Lock #6 were reviewed in 1887 and the contract for the construction was awarded in May of that year. It was determined to increase the lock width to 52' from the 38' width of locks #1-#5 to permit the passage of two-25' barges in a single passage. Assistant Engineer R. S. Burnett was placed in charge of the site. It was the first to be built from the river bottom up by the Corps of Engineers and set the pattern for subsequent structures. The general concept for building a lock and dam from the ground up was a three year period with the work taking place only in the summer and fall when the river was sufficiently low for a cofferdam to protect the work area. The first year was used to quarry the necessary stone, and collect the necessary building materials. The second year was used to construct the lock walls through which the river would be diverted during the building of the dam. Year three was for the construction of the dam. Because of contractor failure, the first three years were consumed in locating and quarrying the necessary stone, and actual construction of Lock #6 did not begin until May 1891.

Assistant Engineer Burnett knew the project was behind and gambled to get it back on schedule. The construction of the lock walls was going so well he determined to proceed with the construction of the dam at the same time. Had there been high water that summer, the work on the dam would have been washed away as there was little place for water go with work under way all the way across the river. Mr. Burnett won his gamble and a hard-earned commendation for completing the 421' long dam and 52' wide lock in the autumn of 1891. Lock #6 was open to navigation on December 2, 1891.

Stone-filled timber cribbing with heavy horizontal planking spiked to the timber cribbing was still the design of choice for the downstream spillway for the dam portion while the locks were made of solid oolitic limestone from Indiana as well as native Kentucky stone. The cofferdam was composed of 206 telephone-pole-size piles driven through the riverbed muck to bedrock. Upon these were wooden stringers spiked; then a line of wooden sheetpiling was driven against them. Mud and clay was heaped upon this wall to give protection of the site up to a rise of seven feet in water level. Much of the masonry work on the lock structure was done by Irish and Italian emigrants and their sons who followed their trade to many such sites across the country. This was the height of the industrial revolution, the time of railroad expansion, the era of the Panama Canal building, and the period in which giant fortunes were generated by men of great vision and few scruples.

Having completed its first dam from the ground up, both the military and civilian personnel began to move upstream with an air of confidence not experienced in the lower structures. While #6 was under construction, they located the upstream spot where #7 would have to be to maintain the needed six foot draft. Steel rods were driven into the muck on river bottom to locate bedrock, and it was found. They generally purchased the permanent-pool land from the landowners, who were very happy to sell as the value of their property would certainly rise with navigable slackwater going through or by it. At the site of #7, however, was a sawmill, owned by one Jedidiah (Dug) Hughes, who was not inclined to sell. The dam would interfere with his ability to capture logs floated downstream to his sawmill and, more importantly, he objected that *during the process of its construction an irresponsible and undesirable class of people would be attracted to the locality, who would make improper use of their premises and be liable to set fire to them.* Since there is little latitude in where a dam can be located for a navigation chain of dams, the Corps was forced, for the first time, to condemn this property. The condemnation proceedings involved some horse-trading in which Dug Hughes was one of the best. He put a price of $1000 per acre on his land at a time when the going price was about $25 per acre. The record of the final price is lost, but it was probably nearer $25 than $1000. Dug took his money, moved his profitable sawmill to the top of the hill behind presentday High Bridge Park, built a log ramp to it, and set about sawing logs again. One of his first major customers was the Corps of Engineers, who needed lumber for the lockmaster houses they were building. History buffs in Jessamine County still speak of Dug Hughes in hushed voices.

The Corps was still building the dams with their own personnel and placed Lieutenant William W. Harts and Associate Engineer John M. G. Watt in charge. Still using rock-filled timber cribbing for the dam, the stone for the lock was moved by an ingenious tramway arrangement whereby the weight of a stone going down was used to pull an empty car up for loading. Excellent photographs taken of the construction of lock #7 show the precise stone work on this structure. The lock was placed in service in 1899, after the second construction season, at a cost of $2 per cubic foot of dam, both of which were records. No record survives of any improper use of the premises by the workmen or fire, as feared by Dug Hughes.

As the 20th century dawned, doubts regarding the viability of the lock/dam system continued to be voiced both on the technical level by Lieutenant Harts and on the economic level by the Corps of Engineers. The railroads had been hauling coal and passengers

BUILDING A MASONRY LOCK

Lock 7 had the best photographic record of the construction of any lock. The pictures on these two pages are from this very complete file by the Corps of Engineers. (Clockwise from lower-left) (1) A wooden cofferdam is built around the lock area with the downstream wall left out. The muck from the river bottom is removed and placed on barges which are pushed downstream and dumped in the river. Platforms are built upon which future steam driven derricks will sit. (2) The enclosure of the coffer dam is then completed and the water pumped out. Wheelbarrows are used to remove the remaining muck to bedrock, upon which the lock walls will be built. (3)

A tramway to carry rock is built around the outside of where the lock walls will be built. Steam-driven derricks are mounted on the platforms, and stones are pushed around the tram to be placed by the derricks. (4) A mid-July 1896 flood submerged the site but (5) by August work resumed. (6, 7, & 8) The upper and lower sills are built, and the inside (9 & 10) of the chamber is lined with smooth stone. The workers (11) proudly pose for the photographer atop their work.

2

4

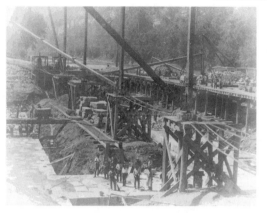

7

9

11

out of the mountains for eight years now much quicker than water could, and their tracks were extending far into the three-forks area where commercial water transportation would be totally impossible. Three days were required to descend a four-barge coal tow from Beattyville to Carrollton. This trip would be about one day by rail with a much larger load. Coal, once on a train, could be shipped to virtually any point in the northern hemisphere while a barge was limited to river ports or reloading. There was still a little timber remaining to be floated down, but the dams were more of a hindrance than a help to this traffic. The two small towns above lock #10, Irvine and Beattyville, had a total population of less than 1000, and would never support a profitable steamboat packet trade. Lieutenant Harts, in a report to the Corps wrote:[11]

> *This cost is so large and the benefits to be obtained depend so much on the capacity of the coal fields and the cheapness of marketing coal, that the question at once arises whether it is certain that the general benefits to the United States will justify the enormous expense. It would be a matter of much chagrin if, upon completion of the system, but little coal should be found or the commerce in coal should be found to be so unprofitable as to make it impossible to compete with other coal regions. The United States would then have an extensive slackwater system on its hands, expensive to maintain, with little or no commerce to justify the expenditure*

The "enormous expense" Lieutenant Harts referred to was about $300,000 per lock and dam or about $2 million to complete the system above #7. If one can shift mental gears and place these sums into the context of year 1900 when a decent wage was less than $1 per day it was an enormous sum indeed and the crystal ball into which Lieutenant Harts gazed was without flaw. His prediction of an economic albatross more than came

BUILDING A TIMBER CRIB DAM

For the most part the timber crib dams were built "in the wet", that is coffer-dams were not built to make a dry pit in which to work. The river bottom muck was dredged to bedrock, but probably still had some silt on top of it. Water, during low flow season, would pass through the rock used to stabilize the timber cribbing. These photos are from the construction of the dam at Lock 7, which was generally typical of timber crib construction in the 1880's and 1890's.

After the length of the dam was dredged to bedrock as well as possible, rows of heavy timbers were placed on the bedrock along the length of the dam for the width of the base. Cross timbers were spiked on these to make a checkerboard of heavy timber. The spikes were 2' long 1" square iron spikes with reverse barbs on them. Once driven, they were very difficult to get out. When the checkerboard (1) got as high as the water line, large rock was placed between the timbers to hold them in place. Just above low waterline (2 & 3) the first "step" was made with heavy wooden planking and the next step up was added. Rock was placed between the timbers as the structure increased in height. Water flowed through the rock-fill as there was no seal on either side of the dam. When the dam was completed (4), wooden "sheetpile" was placed behind the upstream side of the dam. Dirt and gravel was placed behind the sheetpile to form a seal for the dam.

The picture in the lower-right (5) shows the tranquil life of the lockmaster during the golden age of steam travel on the Kentucky River.

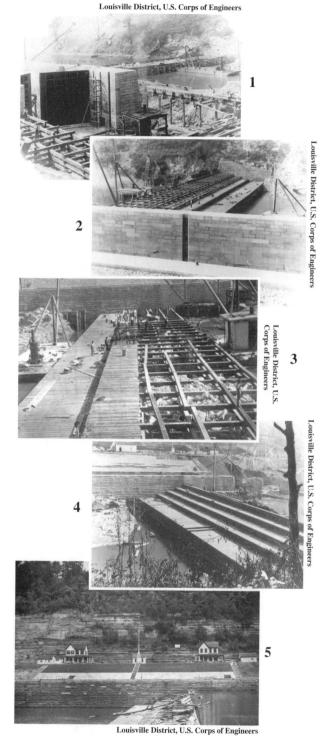

Louisville District, U.S. Corps of Engineers

Louisville District, U.S. Corps of Engineers

Louisville District, U.S. Corps of Engineers

Louisville District, U.S. Corps of Engineers

Louisville District, U.S. Corps of Engineers

true, but Army lieutenants do not set policy on public expenditures. Influential men with extensive holdings in the three-forks area were able to place intense pressure upon both the Kentucky legislature and the congressional political structure to complete the march to the three forks. They continued to hold the 19th-century idea that navigation on the Kentucky River was the key to a profitable three-forks area and were able to convince Congress to continue to fund the projects.

Plans, therefore, continued for a complete slackwater pool to Beattyville with the effective lift between pools increasing from about 15' in the first seven to 18' at Lock 8. With each dam having a lift of 18' from that point to Beattyville, one less lock would be required to reach this goal. Lock #8 was bid to private firms with the low bidder, Thomas A. Sheridan, bidding $261,000 or about $39,000 less than the Corps' estimate. Work went well and the lock put its first boat through on October 15, 1900. Bringing in the 20th Century, this structure marked the end of rock-filled-timber-cribbing dams and masonry locks. All the rest of the locks and dams would be of solid concrete construction.

The engineers began the planning and design of #10, #1 1, and #12 while #9 was under construction under the direction of Major Ernest H. Ruffner of the Cincinnati District office. Major Ruffner increased the height of dams #9 and #10 from a 15' lift to an 18' lift, shook up the office and field staff, designed the dams to be solid concrete rather than the rock-filled timber cribbing of the first eight, and used steel gates rather than wooden ones. William H. McAlpine began his 50 year career with the Corps on Lock/dam #9, a career which ended with a major dam on the Ohio near Louisville being named for him. His career also included work on the Panama Canal and status as an international expert on navigational dams. Original engineering drawings of Lock #9 survive today with Mr. McAlpine's name on them as a Junior Engineer.

LOVE AMONG THE LOCKS

The locks always have been a focal point of local interest. The left photo, probably taken just after the lock was rebuilt in 1881, shows three ladies and one man on top of the wall opposite the lock. The other man apparently had been dispatched to take the picture. The work-boat in the background appears to have a pile-driving rig on it. Note that all the walls are of timber cribbing construction. The other top photo shows these same brave couples walking out on the wooden dam spillway steps.

The bottom photo shows two couples sitting in the rock pile of Lock 7 (about 1896). These are probably workers showing their ladies the results of their labors. These stones are rough and will be trimmed to fit specific needs on the lock.

Louisville District, U.S. Corps of Engineers

Louisville District, U.S. Corps of Engineers

Louisville District, U.S. Corps of Engineers

As Locks # 9 and # 10 were being completed in 1905, severe flooding occurred that "flanked" the lock/dam structure by completely scoring away the shore on the lock side, leaving the lock in the middle of the river. The real reason for the flanking was that the soft bank on the lock side, which had been excavated for the lock construction then refilled and graded to receive pavement or an "esplanade," had not been paved prior to the flood event and was scoured out. The project specifications called for the soft back-filled dirt to *be subject to exposure during winter and spring rains* before placing the protective paving over it. The Corps, however, made the increase in dam height from 15' to 18' the culprit of the disaster and that is what appeared in all the "official" Corps publications. The "flanking" left the lock in the middle of the river with the dam on the far side, then the lock chamber, then about two hundred feet of water to the shore. Auxiliary dams were ultimately built from the lock chamber to the shore of Locks #9 and #10, leaving the lock in the middle of the river. Major Ruffner reduced the height of the dams of #11 through #14 from 18' to 14.5' and increased the effective height of these structures during low water only by the installation of 6' needle or Boule movable structures on top of the dams. Sluice valves were installed through the dams to lower the level of the pools below the crests when the movable structures were being put in place. The movable structures were put up and down each year, and proved such a hazard to the workmen that the design was first modified, then permanently raised to an elevation slightly lower than the original design (including the movable structures). The sluice valve for lowering the pool, however, proved to be of immense value to Life 5 of the river.

With the march to the three-forks now proceeding at double time, Major Ruffner saw that his funds were being drained by the very high maintenance cost of the rock filled-timber cribbing lower dams. They leaked badly, but worse, at each spring major parts

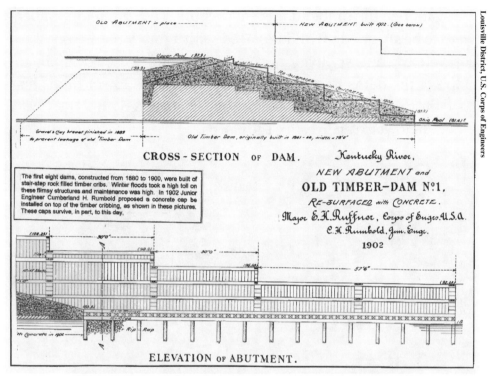

CONCRETE CAP OVER THE TIMBER CRIB DAMS

Maintenance of the timber crib dams was a constant problem to the Corps of Engineers. In 1902 they began a program of removing some of the top wooden steps (shown as the dark stair-step line) and placing a 4' cap of concrete over the timbers, as seen in this drawing. Unfortunately, they used no reinforcing steel in the concrete and the cap ultimately cracked into large chunks. The concrete cap was, however, an improvement over the wooden steps. This drawing shows that wooden guidewalls were still used.

had to be replaced that had been washed out during the previous winter's floods. The Corps of Engineers' reports of the day contain extensive descriptions of the annual destruction of these fairly flimsy structures. As water cascaded down the stair-stepped timber cribbing, it would dislodge the rock within them. Even worse, the timber cribbing itself would rot as it was alternately exposed to water and air. In 1902 Junior Engineer Cumberland H. Rumbold presented an excellent plan to Major Ruffner for placing a concrete cap on the timber dams, and beginning with dam #1 this major renovation to the timber dams was begun. The rotten top timbers were to be stripped off and replaced with a four to eight foot thick concrete cap and spillway, and converted the "stepped" spillway slope of the dams to a smooth slope. All of the lower dams had concrete caps by 1910, which more or less survived until the 1990's when they were repaired by the Corps.

OPENING A LOCK GATE

When first built, most of the locks had wooden gates, were hand-opened, and the gate valves were heavily greased, as seen in this picture. The lock gates, which are in use today, use a large drill motor to open the gates and a hydraulic pump to open the gate valves. The wall valves are still opened by hand, much like this gate is operated.

The contractor working on dam #13 went under after a substantial amount of work was done with the work ultimately being taken over directly by the bonding company. After considerable searching, the bonding company found a superintendent capable of hiring a labor force and completing the job. Most, but not all, mountain folk were glad to see the slackwater pools being built. One particular mountain resident expressed his displeasure of the dam to the new superintendent and this staff with a pistol which was presumed to be loaded at the time. Some bullets flew at night through the resident engineer's office, and the lanterns of the construction inspectors trying to flag trains at night were shot out. The new superintendent, his office staff, and most of the Italian laborers on the job at the time hastily departed for other employment. Another superintendent, staff, and laborers as well as armed guards were employed to complete the job. To the relief of many, the troublemaker soon died of natural causes, and the project was completed in peace.

There was no peace in Washington, however, concerning the funding for the last dam that would place slackwater in Beattyville. This project had the strong scent of pork to the nostrils of Theodore E. Burton, tight-fisted chairman of the powerful House Committee on Rivers and Harbors. As far as he was concerned, the slackwater was near enough the coal fields to float all the coal barges that were likely to be placed upon it, and he deleted funding for lock/dam #14 from the appropriations bill. This deletion was noticed by keen-eyed Kentucky Congressmen, who showed up at a hearing of the Rivers and Harbors Committee with drafts of a bill that would place this line item back. As part of the Committee hearings, the Chief of Engineers requested the opinion of the District Engineer for Kentucky on the matter, who wired back his views very clearly: *In my opinion construction of lock and dam fourteen, Kentucky River, is not advisable. It would promote no public interest if authorized.* Congress, nevertheless, funded the project.

The problems of #14 in Congress were but a prelude of the problems that would be experienced in the field. The chief engineer of the construction firm had extensive experience with part of the Panama Canal construction, but he had a falling out with his partners, left the company, and work on the project virtually ceased.

The Corps declared the project in default, took over direct construction of the project, and completed it.

Lock and dam #14 was placed in service in January 1917 with no celebration of any kind; river traffic had bottomed out. It was a system completed in the 20th-century using 19th-century standards and needs. Even if the system had been conceived in the 20th-century, its design may be little different from its 19th-century design because of the physical limitations of the river: it is very narrow and is very crooked; and it will not float the large barge tows that routinely ply the Ohio and other rivers. The lock chambers on the Ohio River will pass up to 15 large barges in a single lift, while those on the Kentucky will pass but one much smaller barge. The large barge tows on the major rivers that make water transportation very cheap today are not possible on the Kentucky. The easy passage of even a single barge during low water in the early part of the 19th century would, however, have lightened the heart of many would-be coal miners, Bluegrass farmers, and flatboat crews, but railroads had changed everything in the Kentucky River basin.

Like our modern day computers, the navigation system of the Kentucky River was obsolete the day it was completed.

After WWI, when some coal traffic plied the river, public hearing and some investigations were made to extend the slackwater up the North and South Forks, where the major coal fields are. The Corps went through the motions of listening to large landowners of these forks who still felt that water was the cheapest way to get their coal out. After all, there are no toll booths at the locks to pay for the cost of river improvement, but the freight charges of the railroads include the cost of laying the track. The pleas of the businessmen and interested citizens at the public meeting fell upon deaf Corps ears, who at the same time were adding up the annual cost to operate the locks they had. The lock system on the Kentucky River was as high as it would ever go.

CONCRETE LOCK AND DAM CONSTRUCTION

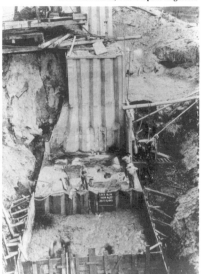

Lock and Dams 9 through 14 were made of solid concrete rather than stone (locks) and timber cribbing (dams) as were 1 through 8. The concrete dams were built in sections, as seen in the construction of dam 13 on the left. The sections were "keyed" together by the four vertical keyways visible on the end of this section, with no reinforcing steel used anywhere in the locks or dams. During the 100 years since these dams were built, they have held together remarkably well considering no reinforcing steel was used.

The photo on the right shows the effects of a rare summer (August 8, 1916) flood during the construction of dam 14. The flood carried away the construction materials on site as well as the railroad tracks used to move construction materials. Water is pouring over the lower coffer-dam built around the section under construction. Other photos of the site showed that the site was cleaned up shortly after the flood receded and work resumed.

Like the concrete dams, the lock walls were constructed in sections using mass, un-reinforced concrete. These photos are of the construction of lock 14 in 1913. The keyways that held the wall sections together are plainly visible in these photos. On-site steam engines are the prime movers just as they were when the first locks and dams were built in the 1840's.

Commerce During the Golden Age

During the march to the Three-Forks, the lower stretches of the river had by far the most commercial activity. Many of the river counties had no rail service, and the river was the only way to move people and goods. Tobacco continued to be the major cash crop for Bluegrass farmers and to the river system itself, but other farm goods such as molasses, hides, cattle, whiskey, and flour appear on manifests of this period. Coal was a major cargo during the winter when it could get out of the three-forks area on high water. Passenger service during this time was mainly local—that is, going from one landing to another then back again—but the river was still a major artery to Louisville and Cincinnati to travelers from river towns.

By chance of history, the system was completed as the United States was preparing for and entering World War I. As with most wars, the infrastructure of the United States was strained to meet the national needs created by the "Great War" this was felt directly by a coal shortage in Frankfort. For whatever reason, the rail system was not able to deliver sufficient coal to keep Frankfort warm in 1917. The river filled this need.

Lock #14 was opened in January 1917, and on February 7, 1917 the Corps of Engineers towboat *Gregory* delivered small barges containing 8,500 bushels of coal. The local paper raised some Frankfort merchants' eyebrows by noting that the coal cost $0.10 per bushel at Beattyville plus $0.03 transportation to Frankfort, or about half the price they had to pay. It is interesting to note that as late as 1917 coal was still quoted by the "bushel," rather than by the ton, indicating that it was intended for fireplace, not industrial use.

It was profitable to provide Frankfort, but not Lexington which is several miles from the river, with fireplace coal during WWI. Valley View, the nearest landing to Lexington, did not have a coal unloading facility nor was there any way to move coal over the road from Valley View at that time. Coal to Lexington could best be shipped by rail directly from the three-forks area. The coal shipment held steady at about 10,000 tons per year through the 1930's and increased some during WWII, just as it had in WWI. Tonnage of this magnitude was for partial supply of power plants and fireplaces, but the river could not come close to supplying all the needs of a major power plant. Power plants had been built on the river for its cooling water, not coal supply. As long as fireplaces used coal there was a small market for it, but when heating moved to gas, oil, and electricity, there was simply no market for small quantities of coal, even at a low price. Shortly after WWII, the coal shipments fell to virtually nothing.

In 1898 the first environmental concerns of the river crept into the Corps of Engineers' annual report. This report states that *the dumping of refuse from stables and sawmills into the river has been stopped*, which indicates that it had been a problem. This report, however, says nothing of direct disposal of municipal sewage into the river or its tributaries, which was common practice in that day. The practice was accepted as the only method to get sewage out of town in the relatively few towns that had public sewers of any kind. All of these were combined storm and sanitary pipes.

For a time, the small amount of oil pumped from the meager fields of the "three-forks" area was barged through the system. The shipment of crude oil, mainly from the fields around Irvine, peaked out in 1925 at over 136,000 tons, but pipelines removed this freight from the water by 1931. The timber had been cut and not replaced. Packet boats ceased serving the Frankfort trade in the 1930's, and the showboats that brought a few magic moments of comedy, drama, and melodrama to the rural river settlements packed away their steam calliopes to museums or watery graves. Recreational boating was by far the major traffic on the River, but that is not the purpose the Corps of Engineers had in mind when it built the system.

Showboats

An unverified, but plausible, story is circulated about the first show-boat on the Kentucky River. At the dawn of showboats, in the mid-19th century, the navigable portion of the Kentucky River wound through very rural Kentucky countryside and machinery of any sort was still something of a novelty to many folk. A farmer and his six year old son were hunting near the banks of the river, when a showboat rounded the bend with its steam calliope at full volume, emitting both sound and sight unfamiliar to rural Kentucky ears and eyes. The farmer, full aware of his Christian duty, blasted away at the varmint. The calliope player, seeing the puffs of smoke and the gun still raised to the farmer's shoulder, raced to the edge of his platform and dived into the water below. In his hasty departure, a valve stuck on the steam instrument and it continued to emit both screech and steam. The little boy looked up at his dad and asked, "Did you kill it, Paw?" The farmer shook his head and said, "Nope, but I sure made the varmint let go of that man."

The varmint was indeed not killed, and showboats brought many magic hours of dreams, tears, and laughs to thousands in the Kentucky River small towns and landings. Names like *The Princess, Prices Floating Opera, The Majestic, Captain Harts Showboat, and the Temple of Health* were well known on the Kentucky while on the larger Ohio and Mississippi *Temple of the Muses, Frenche's New Sensation, Dreamland, Cotton Blossom Pavilion, and Bryants New Showboat* were household names. Their regular stops on the Kentucky River were up as far as Ford (Pool #10) with regular stops at Dix River, Glen Mary, Moxley, Belle Point, Brooklyn, Gilberts Creek, Twin Chimneys and others. When a showboat entered the Kentucky River, it generally spent about two weeks playing at the various stops by going upriver with one play and descending with another before reemerging again into the larger waters of the Ohio River. The actors who made repeated stops at the same places were made, in a manner, "honorary citizens" of the stops and were treated with the table delicacies of the area. Up the Kentucky River it was rabbit, doves, squirrel, quail, and grouse. (In the mining towns of Pennsylvania, where the population had eastern European heritage, the cast was treated with goulash, stuffed cabbage, and borsch.) It was not unknown for a mother to display to the ticket seller a new arrival to the family since the showboat's last visit to the stop.

Between 1831 and the beginning of WWII, at least three dozen showboats played the river towns and landings on the upper Mississippi and Ohio Rivers and their tributaries, as far up as navigation would permit. The "format" of each showboat was different, and was a direct reflection of the personality of the owner of the boat who was also the boat captain, boat pilot, script writer, show producer, show director, actor, part-time ticket sales, public relations director, boat quartermaster, and sometimes physician. During the golden age of showboats, which ended about the beginning of WWI, professional entertainment of any type was virtually unknown to the small towns and landings that dot the Kentucky River shore. The showboat was it, and their arrivals were eagerly awaited by people in the river towns and landings.

The arrival of the showboat was announced in midday by the ever-present calliope as the showboat rounded the bend toward its stop. This was a magic sound to the housewife in the hot kitchen, the farmer pitching hay, and the young people seeking more diversion than Kentucky farms and small towns had to offer. An advance publicist generally had posted announcements of the showboat's arrival, but due to the uncertainty of water conditions and the mechanics of a steamboat, arrivals were not certain until the sound of the steam calliope vibrated from hill to hill. Among the Muses, honored by the Greeks as goddesses of poetry and song, the ninth was the silver-toned *Calliope*. Her name was derived from two Greek words, *kallos* and *ops,* meaning beauty and voice, and she was assumed to preside over the arts of eloquence and epic poetry. Even a Greek muse can probably rotate in her fictional grave at the sound of a steam calliope associated to her name, but this voice was beauty to the ear of the Kentucky River listener.

Each calliope had its distinctive sound, and a keen ear knew the difference between them. Each showboat had its theme song which it played as it approached the dock. Then for the remainder of the afternoon, various familiar tunes such as *There'll Be a Hot Time in the Old Town Tonight* and *Darktown Strutters Ball* were played till show time. This was as near a concert as river towns ever had. Mainly men played these instruments as they took more muscle than most Victorian women's fingers had. The brass keys were directly connected to the steam they controlled, and the use of asbestos gloves while playing was necessary, as were ear plugs. There was no such thing as a showboat without a calliope.

By the theater standards of today, the shows would be considered "hamy," but to the audience of that day, they were a transport into another world, a world far from walking behind a mule, the scrubboard, or the hot wood stove in the kitchen. The show format fell into two broad categories: vaudeville and melodrama. The earliest shows were mostly vaudeville, and from about 1900 drama, of sorts, was added. Vaudeville continued to be inserted between the acts of the drama as the audience would not permit an intermission. They came to be entertained and expected at least two good solid hours of entertainment, with no breaks. Many had spent the better part of an afternoon getting scrubbed and getting there by foot, horse cart, or mule back and had a long ride home late at night. They wanted, and got, their money's worth.

The vaudeville acts were the song and dance, magic shows, a standup comic, and sometimes a serious musician. Little skits, often written by the captain, were interjected between the various acts. Many vaudeville players had real talent and were not just local bumpkins dressed in ill-fitting clothes.

SHOWBOAT MAJESTIC

This showboat was typical of many that brought magic hours of drama, tears, and laughs to Kentucky River audiences. These gangplanks could be dropped at small and large landings or anywhere an audience could assemble.
Like the Majestic, most did not have their own power and had to be towed up and down the river with towboats like the ATTA BOY shown here.

Showboats, however, are best remembered for melodrama: plays with a plot of clear separation between good and evil; between heroine and villain; and between the just and the unjust. Most of the plays had a moral, and the audience was plainly on the side of the good, the heroin, and the just. The audience became completely absorbed into the play, and, contrary to popular opinion, did not routinely cheer the hero(ine) or hiss the villain. That was more widely done by "city" audiences, who had the option of viewing both serious drama and melodrama. Because of its proximity to the underground railroad (Kentucky and Ohio) and the memory of the Civil War still fresh upon the minds of much of the audience, *Uncle Tom's Cabin* was probably the favorite drama along the river for many years. Pushing a close second was *Ten Nights in a Barroom*. In this play the heroine, a girl in her pre-teen years, endeavors to rescue her father from the clutches of demon-rum and with the immortal lyric:[12]

> *Father, dear Father, come home with me now.*
> *The clock in the steeple strikes one.*
> *You promised, dear Father, that you would come home*
> *As soon as your day's work was done.*
> *Come home, come home*
> *Dear Father, dear Father, come home.*

Kentucky audiences no doubt had some personal knowledge of this situation and took it seriously.

Another favorite was *Tess of Storm Country* in which a squatter and his daughter (Tess) eak out a living by illegal fishing. The squatter is wrongly accused of a murder, but in the last act, the real villain is revealed, led off to jail, and Tess's father is freed. The play ends with the cast singing: *"Mine eyes have seen the glory . . . . ."* (Battle Hymn of the Republic). Other typical play titles include: *Her Dead Sisters Secret, Over the Hill to the Poorhouse,* and *No Mother to Guide Her.* This was real stuff to Kentucky River audiences, and they watched and wept without shame.

The heroine was generally the centerpiece of the play, and she had to be able to run, duck, fall, get up, fall again, crawl under a bed, scream, swing by a rope, deliver an uppercut, kick, and still have sufficient breath to say her lines. Heroines were pursued by gangsters, magicians, dope fiends, bull fighters, squatters, assassins, gypsies, and suave villains in long black capes. They had to endure confinement in madhouses, prisons, graves, huts, caves, toolsheds, grandfather clocks, and opium dens. A good heroine had to be of sturdy stock.

Most showboats were family affairs, very much like the Edna Ferber book *"Show Boat,"* later put to music by Jerome Kern under that title. The father was the undisputed master of all. Many of them had river pilots papers for all of the waters they would ply as the cost of a full-time on-board pilot was very high. The father would pilot the boat, select the show or write it, cast it, produce it, direct it, star in it, give it publicity in the stop, purchase food and supplies for the cast and boat crew, and make sure no hanky-panky went on between cast members. The success or failure of the showboat was upon his shoulders, and his financial backers relied upon him.

Next in line of authority, and responsibility, was the mother. Her responsibilities were more earthy, but just as vital to the success of the entire operation. Her duties included wardrobe selection and maintenance, set maintenance, line coaching, general script supervision, and minding the kids. Her most important duty, however, was talent. A showboat captain would be wise to select a wife who could make a real contribution to the production to keep the payroll down by one or two persons. Musical talent as well as acting talent were expected and used. In her spare time, she kept the books and kept track of the money.

From the cradle the kids were part of the show and were expected to be born with talent and a liking for the stage. Betty Bryant, for example, appeared on stage at the age of six weeks as the infant in the arms of the fleeing slave in *Uncle Tom's Cabin*. She ultimately came to know every line of every play her father, Captain Billy Bryant, produced, and she played virtually every female role in all of them at some time in her life. She is still remembered by old timers along the Kentucky River stops where she frequently played. She remains active today in keeping alive the history of the river showboats. It was a real disappointment to the captain and his wife to have kids with no interest or aptitude in the theater.

By any standards, the hired actors were professionals. In the early days of showboats through the height of vaudeville in the early 20th century, the professional stage was a shaky way to make a living. Pay was low, runs were often short-lived, unscrupulous producers would abscond with the gate leaving the cast thousands of miles from home with no money, and the cast generally stayed in rooming houses where the food was bad. On a showboat all this was different. The work was steady, the pay was regular, the food was good, plenty of fresh air existed and the producer had no way to abscond with the gate. The showboat captain had no trouble in selecting a cast, and they often stayed with a boat for many years. Husband and wife teams were preferred as this cut down on certain problems among the cast.

The boat crew, or deck hands, were often conscripted for non-speaking parts, and most loved it. They were also ticket takers, concession sellers (on a commission basis), prop makers, publicity distributors, and any other task that needed doing. A few moved from the role of deck hand to full-time actor, but this was rare. They had plenty to do keeping the boat and the tow running.

Good publicity and a good relationship with the people at each town were key to the success of a showboat. The captain would purchase supplies at almost each stop, pay in cash, distribute passes to the "right people," pay the license fees, make sure his posters were up, shake hands with all who knew him, and make himself very pleasant to the local hierarchy. He wanted no badmouthing about his operation as most shows on the Kentucky River were one-night stands.

Ticket prices were low: about 35 cents for general admission, 50 cents for a balcony seat, and 75 cents for a reserved seat. This was in an era when $15 per week was a livable wage. The size of lock

#1 (38'x145') determined the maximum size of the showboat that could play the Kentucky River. Some that played the Mississippi and Ohio main towns were considerably larger than this. Many showboats had their own full-time tow boat, some had their own power (but this took up space needed for the show), and some hired tows.

One major, but novel accident involving as showboat occurred in pool #7. The tow of the showboat *Princess* was having trouble with a slipping leather drive belt. This drive design called for large leather belts to transmit power from the steam engine to the drive shaft with one belt used for forward movement and a twisted belt for reverse. The belt not in use would be slipped off the drive pulley to an idler and the belt to be used slipped on the drive pulley. A local river hang-about suggested using a special belt dressing, in common use on steam-driven farm equipment in the area, to treat the leather to give it friction on the drive shaft. The key ingredient of this dressing was sorghum molasses. The stuff worked quite well on farm machinery but when it came time to put the boat in reverse, by slipping the drive belt off and the twisted belt on, the forward belt would not slip off the drive shaft. The boat kept on going forward, struck some rocks and sunk. The tow was not damaged and everything of apparent value was removed from the *Princess*. Several houses in the vicinity still have decorative doors later removed from this wreckage before it was raised and towed off.[13]

WWI, better roads, radio, and labor costs combined to bring the era of showboats on the Kentucky River to an end by about 1920. Some survived on the Mississippi and Ohio Rivers, where there were major cities, until WWII. *Bryants New Showboat* played from the Lawrence Street dock in Cincinnati from 1930 until 1942, at which time was sold to the Greene Line and converted to a freight terminal. There are several museums today that have preserved the memories of showboats, including their calliopes and in real life the Captain's daughter sometimes did marry the leading man.

In reality, the decline of the River system began the moment the last lock and dam were completed in 1917, but no one knew it at the time. The rail system into the coal fields of eastern Kentucky was largely in place by the time the concrete hardened on that dam. Railroads made the bulk movement of coal cheaper and quicker than on the small barges that could navigate the tight bends of the Kentucky River and squeeze through its tiny locks.

Life Four

DECAY AND DECLINE
(1932-1988)

If a specific point is needed to set the beginning of the decline
and decay of the River system, it would likely be 1932 when the
Corps of Engineers said, "No more." The Corps was now operating under the 1930 Rivers and Harbors Act, which had more cost
accountability than its 1879 forerunner. Under the Kentucky River
section of the Corps 1932 Annual Report the statement: *The improvement of this locality* (meaning the total Kentucky River system) *other than authorized by the existing project, is not deemed advisable at the present time* appears and is repeated in subsequent Annual Reports. This meant that only the very necessary repairs were
to be made to the locks and dams. They were not to be improved.
Other similar river systems such as the Little Miami in Ohio were
likewise categorized. In spite of the small amount of commercial
traffic on the river at this time, certain interests wanted to continue
the extension of the slackwater system past Beattyville into the
forks. The Corps said it would perform only those things needed
to maintain what it had, but "No more!" The general practice was
then to perform heavy maintenance on one or two locks per year,
meaning that once each 10 years or so each lock would receive
heavy maintenance, and then only as little as could be done. Most
of the work was done on the locks and their mechanisms, with the
dams largely untouched, except for placing derrick stone down-

stream of the spillways to slow undercutting of the dam structure. Most of the stone so placed was too small and was washed away in a season or two.

The listing of the tonnage carried on the river could be deceiving. The 1930 tonnage was listed as 111,186 tons, and the 1932 tonnage was 227,261. Most of the 1932 tonnage, however, was sand and gravel through the lower locks only plus some building material for short term building projects in the upper river. A small amount of coal was shipped from the three-forks area to the power plants on the river, but this was only a trifle compared to the total shipped to them by rail. In the summer of 1936 the movable "A-Frame" gates on dams #12 and #13 were not put in place as there was no navigation on these pools that required this depth of water. By 1951 the listed tonnage was down to 66,448 tons, almost all of which was sand and gravel in the lower locks.

The maximum barge tow that could navigate the river bends was two "regular" barges and a "short" barge so that the short barge plus the towboat (pusher) could go through the lock as a unit. The maximum size barge must fit into the smallest lock (38' x 145') on the river. (Most commercial barges today are about twice that size.) Each barge had to be pushed into the lock chamber, disconnected from the tow, the tow would back off, the barge moved up or down in the lock chamber, and floated out. The process was repeated for each barge on the tow. After lockage was completed, the tow was reunited and proceeded to the next lock. The process took at least an hour at each lock, provided nothing went wrong. Travel time between the locks was 2 to 4 hours, depending on the pool, bends, current, and other factors. A minimum of three days was required for the trip between Beattyville and the Ohio River, provided the River was not flooding and all of the locks were working. One day was required for this journey by rail, and rail travel was generally unaffected by acts of nature.

The other potential for bulk cargo on the Kentucky River was oil. There is a small amount of oil in eastern Kentucky that had a sufficient market value to justify a pipeline, against which barges could not compete for the same reasons that coal barges could not compete against railroads. Various major oil companies hauled small amounts of oil or gasoline on various parts of the river through WWII. Most of these centered around Estill County, but there were some facilities in Frankfort for the movement of oil. Pipelines took all of the petroleum off the river by 1947.

The decay and decline of the river as a vital transportation artery to the Bluegrass is visualized by comparing the navigation charts from different eras. The navigation chart published in 1942 and updated through 1961 shows seven "landings" (e.g. Peytons Ldg.) between miles 45 and 61 where passengers or freight could be taken on or discharged as needed. The landing names were after the major farms in the area, but they were available to anyone who cared to use the landing. The names of all of the landings have disappeared from the 1987 chart as they and the packets that once served them have vanished.

Through WWI and the years immediately after, rural secondary Kentucky roads were still mud streaks atop farmland. Whether on horseback, buggy, or Model T, going anywhere on them was not taken lightly, and river packet travel was the preferred mode if one were going to or from anywhere near the river. There was no question about the preferred method of hauling heavy freight such as tobacco that had access to the river: the river was it. Improved secondary roads and improved cars and trucks, beginning in the mid 1920's, slowly began to beat out river transportation for short hauls, but packets continued to ply the Kentucky River hauling both passengers and cargo from Kentucky River landings to Cincinnati and Louisville. The death knell of the packet was the 1937 flood. This flood, the largest on record in most of the Ohio Valley, devastated everything along the Kentucky and other rivers. All of the landings were wiped out. All transportation on the river came to a total halt while the water remained high. When the water receded in several weeks, the packets simply did not return like before the flood. The few who tried to revive the service soon found their regular passengers and cargo traveling overland. Only the special cruise and pleasure boats remained. The scheduled packet trade for passengers and cargo was over. The Corps of Engineers cartographer who put the various landings on the 1942 navigation chart was living in the past.

> Kentucky is known for interesting place names such as Black Gnat, Gravel Switch and Rooster Run, and the 1942 Corps of Engineers cartographer made his contribution in sustaining this image. The story goes that Capt. Jack Eversole was towing two barges of coal from Beattyville to Ford one hot summer night and was negotiating the very tight bend at Ross Creek at MP 236 in pool #12. The cook came up from below to cool off a bit and asked the Captain the name of the place he was squirming through. He was in no mood to be a tour guide for his cook and hollered back: "Tight Ass Pop Corn". This exchange ultimately reached the ears of the Corps of Engineers cartographer and a sand bar at MP 236 is duly labeled "T.A.P.C." on the official 1942 Navigation Chart.[2]

The cost to keep the system open was substantial. Each lock had two full-time lockmasters who lived in the very adequate housing provided for them and their families at each lock. (Few of these survive to this day.) Maintenance crews operated out of the shops in Frankfort. Dredging was done on a regular basis to keep the channel depths at the six foot level guaranteed by the Corps of

Engineers. Most of the dredging was done around the locks after the winter floods deposited silt around the lock structures, but sometimes the channel itself had to be dredged. The lock valving and gate operating devices were complex and required constant attention. Routine operation and maintenance costs were from $200,000 to $300,000 per year, a substantial sum in the 50's and 60's. No work other than that absolutely necessary was done to the locks or dams. All Annual Reports cite the decaying state of the structures, but that was the end of the Corps' efforts.

The hub of the maintenance system for the locks and dams on the Kentucky River was Frankfort at Lock #4. This substantial facility was complete with a machine shop, foundry, dredges, work boats, dry dock for the Corps of Engineers work boats, and qualified people to operate everything or fix anything broken. The staff at Frankfort reported to the Ohio Valley Corps of Engineers office in Cincinnati. By either Ohio or Mississippi River standards, the Kentucky River tonnage was just a small cipher on very large page, and the cost of keeping up the Frankfort shops was out of proportion to the tonnage it served. Corps of Engineers auditors long wanted to close their books on this cost, but Kentucky politics had kept them open. Finally, in 1935 the Corps packed up and moved out of Frankfort to Cincinnati, at night,[3] just like the Baltimore Colts did when they moved to Indianapolis. The Corps was taking no chances of being interfered with on this move. Crews were then sent from Cincinnati to the Kentucky River to perform the needed maintenance. When the Corps office in Louisville was opened, the operation of the Kentucky River was transferred there.

World War II brought a slight increase in traffic on the river, but little real maintenance. After the war, the Corps continued to operate the locks on a full-time basis, just as though there were real commercial traffic on the water, but most of the traffic was pleasure craft, for which the Corps had little stomach and less funds.

DECAYED LOCKS

The Corps of Engineers has repaired all of the dams in recent years, but none of the lock chambers. These photos show the decayed condition of the lock chambers, for which repair is needed.

The only real commercial traffic on the river that continued into the 21st century was a three-times-per-week sand and gravel barge tow in the lower four pools. Captain John Donaldson, of Jessamine County, hauled sand and gravel for the Central Kentucky Sand and Gravel of Frankfort until he sold the operation to the Frankfort firm in 1990, which continues to operate the barges. The barges load river-run sand and gravel on the Ohio river downstream from Carrollton and deliver it to Frankfort. This journey of about 75 river miles takes about 11 hours each way. The economy of water transportation for this enterprise, however, made the difference between profit and loss for the sand and gravel company. This, of course, was the intent of the system from the beginning, but few other commercial operations fit this pattern of hauling.

Good use was made of the River in 1973 for the construction of the I-75 Kentucky River bridge. The major pieces of steel were hauled up river much cheaper and in larger sections than could be hauled by highway.

In 1975 an aborted attempt was made to once again haul coal on the river. Two barges were loaded with coal in Beattyville, bound for the Ohio River. For a reason not clear now, a tow was made with one barge through lock #9 and the barge was tied to the lower lock wall while the tug went back upstream for the other barge. While the tug was away, a heavy rainfall occurred in the upper basin causing a major rise in the river stage, lifting the barge tied up at #9 off its ties, and it began to float downstream in pool #8. The barge owner quickly hired a helicopter and deposited a crew member on the loose barge with the hope that he could throw a rope around something and stop the barge from going on downstream. The crew member quickly saw that this was not a good idea and flapped his arms to be taken off the barge, which he was. The floating barge continued to ride the flood crest downstream and eventually came to rest in a flooded soybean field. The barge company made no move to extract its barge from the middle of the soybean field, so the soybean farmer went into the coal business and sold all the coal in the barge. When this was gone, he cut up the barge and went into the scrap iron business. No more coal has been towed on the Kentucky River since that time.[4]

The major casualty of the period of decay and decline was the dam structures themselves, probably for two reasons: they were difficult to work on, and as long as they did not fall in, why fool with them? The lower eight structures were timber cribbing structures that had only a top layer of concrete over the rock-filled timbers. This concrete layer began to come off some of the dams during this period, exposing the timbers underneath, but few cared as long as the pools were maintained. The upper six dams were solid concrete, but underscoring was taking its toll on them as well as on the abutments. The dam abutments also began to crack and fall apart, but the locks continued to operate. The approaches to the locks, most of which were built on timbers, began to fail and lean. Very large amounts of money were required to fix all of this, but the Corps was beginning to tire of pouring good money after bad, with no prospect in sight of major commercial traffic on the Kentucky River ever happening again.

The importance of the Kentucky River system to the Corps can be followed by the space given to it in its Annual Report. During the late 19th century when the system was under full construction, the Kentucky River occupied 15 to 25 pages in the Annual Report with complete copies of important documents included among these pages together with detail cost breakdowns of the various project components. These pages were gradually diminished as Kentucky River projects became operational and their importance to the Corps became negligible. By the 1970's the Kentucky River system occupied a few paragraphs on a single column of the Annual Report, most of which was copied from the previous year. The few important things that did happen, like the lockmaster class action suit against the Corps (see Life 5), did not even make print. Nobody took the trouble to write anything new. In 1953 the first hint that the Corps wanted to bail out, however, did make print: *Operation of Locks #8 - #14 is contingent upon the development of sufficient traffic in this reach of waterway to justify maintenance of navigation.* Sufficient traffic to justify maintenance, of course, did not develop.

Lockmaster Life During the Decline

By the first quarter of the 20th century, the Corps of Engineers was operating many commercial river systems all over the country and had their procedures well in place. Though the commercial traffic on the Kentucky River was minuscule, the operation of the locks in general and the lockmasters who operated them in particular acted as though it were a "real" commercial river. Detailed records were kept in accordance with Corps standards, and the lockmasters went about their duties in a very professional manner. Children of the lockmasters laughed and played at their well- built homes, and housewives gossiped across well-cut lawns. A typical entry in the logbook of Lockmaster John A. Walters at Lock #10 for Monday, March 1, 1943 reads:[5]

Gage 12.2 - 10.0 Term 22o Prec. 00 Weather fair

The weather has been fair all day changing to cold in late afternoon. Roud Smith, handyman, and John Glover, carpenter, came about 11:30 AM on truck driven by Barrett Sullivan who brought lumber, cement, sand and stone to repair breaks in pavement. The truck then went to McClanahans landing and unloaded wickets for lower gate. Overseer Sam Eversole, Junior Aubrey and Diver Joe Brady came later. Lockmaster pruned trees, cleared grounds. Lockmaster cut undergrowth along fencing and assisted in unloading and storing material to repair break in pavement.

When locking actually took place, the log book notes the name of the vessel and what type it was. The "heavy" usage months were in the summer, from May through September. In 1935, for example, the Lock #10 log shows about 30 to 50 lockages per month during the summer, but by 1941 this figure had dropped to 12 to 14 per month, most of which were pleasure craft. Only one lockage took place at Lock #10 during January, February, March, and December of that year. Lockmaster life was good. They kept busy, but not from locking boats through.

Flood Control

During the 1930's, when major public works were being conceived and funded, the Kentucky River was a prime candidate. The 1937 flood was the worst in recorded Ohio Valley as well as Kentucky River history. The downtown areas of Frankfort, Irvine, and Beattyville were under several feet of water for days. Headwater communities, all of which are in the floodplain, were paralyzed. Screams went to Washington for permanent flood relief. TVA was gearing up. Large floodwater storage reservoirs were the answer to flooding problems. Environmental laws concerning such projects were in the distant future.

In 1938 these storage reservoirs were listed by the Corps of Engineers for further study:

Jessamine Creek Reservoir	Main Stem	$10.8 million
Boonesville Reservoir	South Fork	$ 3.9 million
Buckhorn Reservoir	Middle Fork	$ 2.6 million
Laurel Branch Reservoir*	North Fork	$ 1.7 million

*later moved downstream to Walker Creek

WWII, of course, halted these, as well as all other major public works in the country. At the war's end all of these except Laurel Branch continued to be listed and studied. Reservoirs were considered to be regional projects as they, in theory at least, benefited everything downstream. Two local projects were added to the list in 1947:[7]

Cutoff the oxbow of the North Fork at Jackson	$161,000
Construct floodwalls at Frankfort	$ 1.7 million

New projects were added to the list in the 1960's:

Carr Fork (Creek)	Tributary to the North Fork	$45.7 million
Red River	Tributary to the main stem	$34.0 million
Station Camp Creek	Tributary to the main stem	$50 million

The final disposition of these projects is:

Buckhorn Reservoir was placed in operation in the early 1960's at a cost of $11.8 million. It gives some flood relief to Beattyville.

Booneville Reservoir was delisted in the middle 1970's because of cost, environmental problems, and small benefits. Its final cost estimate was $53 million.

Jesamine Creek Reservoir was delisted in the early 1960's at a cost of $46.9 million

Jackson oxbow cutoff was made.

Walkers Creek Reservoir (began as Laurel Branch) was delisted in the late 1960's.

Frankfort floodwalls were broken into three separate projects, of which two have been constructed

Red River Reservoir was delisted, mainly for environmental reasons, in the middle 1970's at a final estimate of $34 million.

The Red River gorge is one of the prime Kentucky hiking, camping, and environmental treasures and was the focus of national attention when a reservoir was proposed within it. **Supreme Court Justice Douglas** led one of the protest marches through the gorge which was probably a leading factor in the delisting. The reservoir would actually have had little effect on the environment within the gorge.

Station Camp Creek Reservoir was to have served as both a flood control and water supply reservoir. It was delisted for environmental reasons as the Station Camp Creek basin is pristine and contains several rare plant and animal species.

The two reservoirs built on the Kentucky River, Buckhorn and Carr Creek, take a small bite off the tops of the floods at Beattyville and Hazard respectively but do not provide anything like real flood control for these cities. The flood walls at Frankfort provide protection for the areas they control, which is a large part of the City. Except for more flood walls in Frankfort, it is unlikely that further major flood protection works will appear on the horizon: there is no place to store the water that comes down the Kentucky River during a flood. Environmental as well as cost considerations make the future construction of major reservoirs a thing of the past.

Conception of the Rebirth

Even as the use of the river was declining as a navigation highway, the conception of its rebirth was under way as a major supplier of drinking water for the municipalities along its banks. First, the towns immediately adjacent to the main-stem river banks tapped it for their drinking water source: Frankfort, Beattyville, and Irvine. Three-forks towns such as Jackson and Hazard continued to use individual wells until the mid-20th century. Following the drought of 1930, Lexington built a major intake in pool 9 and a pipeline to the river. Other cities such as Winchester, Richmond, and Lancaster not immediately on the river later built intakes and pipelines to the river to meet their water supply needs. All of the intakes for these municipalities were built with the assumption that the pools created by the locks and dams would always be there. Without the locks and dams, their intakes would be high and dry. No thought was given by these cities that anything would ever happen to the locks and dams. They were just part of nature as far as they were concerned. As far as the Corps of Engineers was concerned, the locks and dams were barrels of red ink.

The Corps Bails Out

The mission of the Corps of Engineers in the 1970's was to provide flood control and a waterway for commercial traffic. It was not in the business of municipal water supply, as the Kentucky River had become. When commercial traffic ceased, the Corps viewed its mission ended. In the late 1970's the Corps initiated talks with Kentucky seeking the state's commitment to take over maintenance and operation of the lock/dams #5-#14. The ongoing sand and gravel barge traffic of locks #1-#4 was the only thing that kept the Corps from including them in the conversation as the Corps is obligated to keep a lock system open as long as viable commercial traffic exists. Kentucky naturally resisted the Corps' overture since the cost of keeping the system operating is large and there was and is no lockage fee for passage through the locks. The cost of operating and maintaining the decaying locks and dams would have to come from the pockets of all Kentuckians, most of whom vote. Congress explained its position to Kentucky officialdom more clearly in 1981 by appropriating no more funds to operate the system. In 1982 the Corps welded shut Locks #5 through #14 and placed them in "caretaker status".

The decision of the Corps to close the locks was actually sealed during the 1970's by the lockmasters. A class action suit for overtime pay was filed and won out of court by the lockmasters during this period. Their contention was that they were on duty or on call 24 hours a day while living in the lockmaster houses, but were paid for only eight hours per day. If at any time of day or night a boat wanted to lock through, they were obligated to perform the lockage operation.[9] Never mind that most of the time there was no lockage of any kind taking place, they were still on duty. The award to the lockmasters amounted to several million dollars with one to two hundred thousand dollars awarded to lockmasters with many years of service, a handsome sum to a federal employee in the 1970's. The Corps wanted to seal this hole into which their money was being poured.

While the number of persons who wanted to continue to use the Kentucky River for recreation was not vast, they can be vocal and many of them had influence in county courthouses as well as the Statehouse. With something of a suspicious eye upon each other, Kentucky (acting through its Natural Resources and Environmental Protection Cabinet) and Corps officials hammered out and signed a <u>Memorandum of Understanding</u> dated 22 February 1985 the purpose of which reads as follows:

> *1. Purpose: The purpose of this Memorandum of Understanding (hereinafter referred to as "MOU") is to establish general relations and procedures under which the Commonwealth of Kentucky (hereinafter referred to as the "STATE") and the U.S. Army Corps of Engineers (hereinafter referred to as the "CORPS") will (1) implement a lease agreement for renewed operation and maintenance of Locks and Dams 5 through 14 on the Kentucky River, (2) define the support role and maintenance obligations of the Corps, and (3) determine the respective rights, duties and responsibilities of the STATE and the CORPS, pending proposed divestiture by the United States.*

The *pending proposed divestiture by the United States* clause, meaning complete ownership of locks/dams #5-#14 by the Commonwealth, was taken in the text of the MOU to occur on or before 15 October 1988 (later extended to 15 October 1989), a very optimistic date, but like any shotgun wedding, the fathers of the bride and groom (Federal and State governments in this case) were not inclined to put the ceremony off. The text also provided for "major maintenance" to be done by the Corps prior to the transfer. The original process of transferring the first five locks/dams from the State to the Federal government in the 1880's took about one year. This reverse process has now been under way since 1988, and as of winter 2001 a single lock/dam (#10) has actually been transferred to the Commonwealth. It proves the ancient proverb: *"It is easier to get into something than to get out of it."*

THE LAST COMMERCIAL RUNS
ON THE KENTUCKY RIVER

The last commercial use of the Kentucky River was to haul sand and gravel from the Ohio River near Carollton to Frankfort through locks 1-4.   The run was a three-barge tow with two of the barges made to exactly fit into a lock chamber and the third barge together with the towboat would fit as a unit into the lock chambers. One barge at a time could be locked through, a process that took about an hour per lock. These pictures show the tow going to the Ohio River for the next load of sand and gravel. The photo on the bottom right is Captain John Donaldson (back to camera) on the towboat Sam Dreyer *with the Author, who was making this run with Captain Donaldson.*

The Corps was more anxious to remove this money-eating albatross from its neck and payroll since it fit not one bit into its mission of flood control or maintaining commercial waterways. The State, on the other hand, saw that these pools had to be maintained as about 600,000 persons depended upon them for water for themselves and the industries that provided their subsistence. The pools were also a major point of recreation for those persons who fished, water skied, and plied their houseboats on its waters. Both sides knew well that the 100-year old rickety dams and decaying locks had to be renovated at a cost of many millions of dollars to someone.

While the terms of the Memorandum of Understanding were being hammered out, a lease agreement between Kentucky and the Corps was entered into, and the locks were reopened to weekend summer boaters in 1985 at the expense of the State.

When the Corps first announced its intention to close the lock system in 1981, the State appointed a Kentucky River Task Force, the forerunner of several such bodies that had noble titles, but no money or authority to do anything. Other such bodies were created by the Legislature, but no real action was taken by the State except to operate the locks during the summer weekends and do just enough maintenance to keep them open. In 1986 the Kentucky River Authority, a body politic,[10] was created to receive the Lock/dams #5 through #14 from the Corps as set up in the Memorandum of Understanding. It was endowed with no staff, no operating money but with the power to issue bonds for the capital maintenance of the structures and the power to assess water withdrawal fees to retire the bonds sold for capital costs. Appointment of the board members was contingent upon ownership of the structures by the Commonwealth, a prospect in 1986 that was nowhere in sight so no one was appointed. The Authority did not meet until 1990.

At this point, things did not look good for the Kentucky River: State and Federal bureaucrats were endlessly debating fine points of a memo with no end in sight; there was no money to do anything; the locks that had once been open all the time were now open only a few days a year; the locks and dams who nobody wanted plainly needed major repair; and it was absolutely necessary that they be maintained for water supply. The Rebirth of the Kentucky River is the drama that unfolds in Life 5.

Life Five
THE RIVER REBORN
A DRAMA ON THREE STAGES
(1988 onward)

The rebirth of the Kentucky River is a three-stage drama: the audience (persons who live in the Kentucky River basin) is viewing a play with three stages, upon each of which are separate actors and a separate script, but with a common theme – the rebirth of the Kentucky River. The audience is straining to hear the lines from each stage and see how it relates to the lines from the other stages. A single actor, the Kentucky River Authority, moves from stage to stage to say its lines there and move to the next stage, or remain silent for a while. Sometimes a stage is darkened to be re-lit again as the plot unfolds.

The fifth life of the Kentucky River was not even a twinkle in the eye of Engineer Welsh and the other men who conceived the original lock and dam system and guided its birth. The present life has the prospect of bringing far more prosperity to central and eastern Kentucky than a water transportation system ever could, but is in reality a step-child of the original intent of the lock and dam system: **municipal water supply.**

Due partly to the rugged terrain through which the Kentucky River wanders, partly due to the chance location of early settlements in Kentucky, partly to avoid Indian attacks from the rock shelters near the river, and partly due to the frequent and severe

MUNICIPAL WATER INTAKES

Shown here are two of the twelve municipal water intakes on the Kentucky River from Carrollton to Beattyville. These systems provide water to about 600,000 persons. In order for these intakes to function, the pools must be maintained. In addition, there are four electric power plants as well as other industries that use Kentucky River water in their production process.

At left is the Kentucky-American Water Company intake in Pool 9 serving Fayette County and parts of adjacent counties.

Above is the City of Winchester water intake immediately above Dam 10.

flooding of the river, there are only three towns located directly on the Kentucky River below the forks: Frankfort, Irvine, and Beattyville. As municipal water systems began to develop, these river towns, as well as other close towns, looked to the Kentucky River pools as a sure water supply. Their intakes were designed to use the deep pools created by the dams, and it was assumed they would always be there. Water intakes need to be several feet below the surface of the water to function properly, not just the few inches that would be available during the summer without the dams and the resulting pools.

On Stage One: The Corps Moves On and Out

On this stage there are but two original actors: the Corps of Engineers and the agent of the Commonwealth of Kentucky: the Cabinet for Natural Resources and Environmental Protection (NREP). They are undergoing the shotgun wedding that began in Life Four. The audience cheers for offspring from this union in the form of stable, operable locks and dams on the Kentucky River. A third actor, the Kentucky River Authority, makes a later appearance upon this stage.

The couple has bickered over the exact meaning of the terms "major maintenance" and "operating order" in the Memorandum of Understanding (MOU). The Kentucky NREP was eyeing the locks and dams and saw that the Corps of Engineers was doing very little to provide the major maintenance they understood the *Memorandum of Understanding* specified. The dams built on timber cribbing (Dams #5-#8) were in particularly bad condition, and water was also pouring through the lock gates. Underscoring was taking place under the toe of the dams, and the walls in the lock chambers were flaking badly. The lock approaches were falling in, and some of the mass concrete was badly cracked. The definition of "operational condition" and "major maintenance" specified in the *Memorandum of Understanding* was viewed very differently in Frankfort and the Corps headquarters. The state could see that an immense sum was required to fix this. The Federal government, on the other hand, has no further use or need for this decaying system of locks and dams and wants them out of their way and out of their pocketbook. Each side hopes that the other will come up with the money to make the union bliss-filled.

Wanting to place as little drain on the State coffers as possible in repairing the locks and dams, the State in 1989 and again in 1991, filed two law suits against the Federal Government and the Corps of Engineers stating basically that the Corps had not followed the word and intent of the *Memorandum of Understanding*. The State lost both of these court battles, but in a sense, won the war through Congressional funding for the repair of the dams over the next several years. For a few months in 1989 it appeared that the transfer of the lock and dam system to the state would bog down. The state, of course, was unwilling to pay the Federal government any cash money for them as they were far more of a liability than an asset. The Federal government (General Services Administration), on the other hand, said this was valuable property and the Federal government was not in the habit of giving away valuable property to anybody. Notices, handbills, and a sign were actually issued for the sale of Lock 6 with its property. Cooler heads prevailed and the sale was withdrawn before its actual date. It is uncertain what a private individual would have done with a lock and dam, if this sale had gone through to an individual.

AUCTION OF LOCK 6 PROPERTY

While the Corps of Engineers and the Commonwealth of Kentucky were playing "chicken" over the transfer of Lock and dams 5 through 15 in 1989 – 1991, the Corps actually placed the property of Lock 6 on the open market through this auction. The auction was pulled a few days before it actually took place. One cannot help but wonder what would have happened if this property had actually been sold to a private individual.

The lawsuits against it notwithstanding, the Corps was still anxious to rid itself of this albatross and did what they could to comply with the terms of "major maintenance" and "operational condition" through this Congressional funding. In various bills, Congress ultimately appropriated about $15 million for the stabilization of the dams only. No Congressional funds were established for repair of the leaky locks. The dam stabilization took place between 1993 and 2001. The major components of the dams (dams #5-#14) were stabilized with sheet piling and concrete. A concrete barrier was placed across the lock chamber of locks #11-#14 to stabilize the shaky lock walls and prevent leakage during low water. Whereas these barriers deliver the positive benefit of lock stabilization and leak prevention, they do, however, eliminate any navigation through the lock, forever.

When dam stabilization was taking place, low level water release valves were installed in dams #11-#14. These valves, when opened, permit the release of water from the upper pools to the lower pools thereby giving the lower pools the benefit of the water stored in the upper ones during a drought. These were paid for by the Kentucky River Authority at a cost of less than $50,000 each. These valves are a major asset to the Reborn Life of the Kentucky River and mark the first real achievement in increasing the supply of available water on the river during a drought. They were successfully used during the 1999 drought.

The official transfer of the lock and dam system has proven to be more difficult than any attendee of the 1986 shotgun wedding ever dreamed. The difficulty has been not with the condition of the locks and dams, which has been settled, but with the ground pollution around the lockmaster houses. These houses, most of which are about 100 years old, have been painted and repainted with lead-base paint. This paint has washed off and contaminated the surrounding ground. Before the state will accept the locks and

TIMBER CRIB DAM REPAIR IN THE 1990'S

In anticipation of turning the Kentucky River lock and dam system turn-over to the state, the Corps of Engineers made extensive repairs to them in the 1990's, as seen in these photos. The 4-foot thick concrete cap placed over the timber cribbing in the early 1900's was not reinforced and had broken into large chunks. Since there was no concrete behind the dam's upstream face, water could pass through the middle of the dams. To repair these dams the Corps drove a row of sheet piling behind the dams, filled the space between the sheet piling and the dam with gravel and concrete, pumped concrete grout into the voids within the timber cribbing, and replaced the concrete cap with new, reinforced concrete. These photos show the deteriorated condition of the dams as well as the completed new spillway.

dams, the Federal government must clean up this contamination to a certain level. This means hauling off contaminated dirt, adding clean dirt, or a combination of both—at a very substantial cost. As of this writing (2001) only lock and dam #10 has been totally cleaned up and transferred to the state. It is hoped that by the end of 2001 the remaining properties of lock and dam #5 - #14 will be transferred. The lockmaster houses (except #10) have been torn down, bad dirt hauled off, good dirt hauled in, and grass planted.

The lights on this stage are dimmed, but not off. The next major scene upon this stage will be the transfer of locks #1-#4 to the state. When locks #5-#14 were considered for transfer, there was a viable commercial traffic in sand and gravel from the Ohio River to Frankfort (Lock #4), and the Corps kept them open for that purpose. This traffic has since slowed considerably, and rumblings are again heard about their transfer to the state. Because these locks and dams have been used for recent commercial traffic, the Corps has kept them in much better condition than those where commercial traffic long ago ceased, but they are by no means in mint condition. When this transfer takes place, the lights on this stage will be permanently turned out.

On Stage Two - The Lexington Problem*

In the spring of 1988 Mother Nature strode upon this stage and tweaked the nose of the Kentucky River municipal users with a drought. In hindsight it was really a *small timer* except for the first two weeks of July when the flow in the river at the Lexington intake bottomed out at 78 million gallons per day, or just slightly more than the needs of Lexington. Compared to the drought years of 1929-30, when the flow at the Lexington intake reached about 6 mgd, the 1988 drought was just a wakeup call. There were several bothersome things about this drought, however: when a drought

*In this context "Lexington" means all of Fayette County plus the parts of the adjacent counties served by the Kentucky American Water Company.

REPAIR OF CONCRETE DAMS

In preparation of the transfer of the locks to the State all the dams including the concrete ones were repaired by the Corps of Engineers. This repair consisted of driving sheetpile behind the dam, repair of the holes and the face of the dam, and placing concrete and gravel between the sheetpile and the dam upstream face. In Locks 11-14 a water release valve was installed and a bulkhead was placed across the lock chamber on the upper sill.

is going on, no one knows how long it will last; it was following the pattern of the 1930 drought until rains came in the middle of July (rain did not come in the 1930 drought until the end of November); water withdrawal permits required that a very large amount of water continue to flow past the intakes; there is no available storage of water in the river since the water stored in the fourteen pools could not be accessed; and the infrastructure (pumping and treatment capacities) of some of the utilities was not adequate to meet their demands during spring and early summer when lawns and gardens cry for water. The most bothersome thing, however, was that the Kentucky River revealed itself to be an unreliable source of water.

Lexington (Fayette County) accounts for about one half of the water used from the Kentucky River and about 90% of the problems. Some of the problems are acts of nature, but many of them are self-inflicted. Few of them seem to want to go away.

The rebirth of the Kentucky River actually began on November 30, 1988, at 8:30 am when Lexington Mayor Scotty Baesler convened the Regional Meeting on Water Supply Planning for Central Kentucky/Kentucky River Basin. At this meeting Mayor Baesler discussed the drought from which Kentucky River users had just emerged and proposed to do something about it. He proposed to set up a Kentucky River Basin Steering Committee, that would investigate ways to do something about the Kentucky River to make it a reliable source of water. The funding for the investigation would come from the City ($100,000) and the Kentucky American Water Company ($125,000). Mayor Baesler appointed 30 persons to the Steering Committee from the ranks of local leaders, water professionals, and the environmental community. The first meeting was January 19, 1989.

In a large-sized working group like this it is natural that unofficial schools of thought would emerge. In this case, some consisted of only one or two Steering Committee members, and in some cases five or ten members would share the same concepts for fixing the Kentucky River. In general these schools of thought were: the conservationist/environmentalist, who wanted to solve the problem by cutting back on water use and building little new; the builders, who wanted to build new, large dams; the pragmatics who wanted to fix the existing locks and dams and use that water; the boaters who wanted to make sure the locks stayed open for recreational boating; and the dreamers who proposed very novel devices and uses of the river. In the end, some of these concepts merged.

For the next several months the Steering Committee heard from local and regional persons and agencies that had some knowledge of the Kentucky River and what could be done about it to make it a secure water source for central Kentucky in general and Lexington in-particular. These presenters set forth a very wide variety of concepts as to what could be done on or to the river. Persons and agencies who had worked with river basins elsewhere also told the Task Force the techniques they had used in similar conditions.

After hearing all of this, the Steering Committee listed about twenty-two concepts that might be applicable to the Kentucky River. They then went over them one by one to select a "short list" of three concepts that would be examined in more detail by a consultant. The proposed "long list" concepts included dredging, new large dams, pumping up the river from the Ohio River, crest gates on the existing dams, conservation with nothing new, pipeline to other lakes like Lake Cumberland, develop Eagle Creek in Scott County, and many, many more. The three which emerged on the "short list" were: a pipeline using Ohio River water (either treated or untreated), small upstream reservoirs, and a large dam above pool 9 (location of the Lexington intake). The concept set forth by Steering Committee member David Blythe and retired engineer Virgil Proctor was to stabilize the existing locks and dams and use the water they store. This concept was dismissed by the Steering Committee but has been put into effect and has been the lifesaver on the river today.

After several rounds of proposals and interviews, the Steering Committee selected a team of engineers led by Harza Engineering Company of Chicago. Harza was bound by their contract to study only the three concepts the Steering Committee had selected. In July 1991, Harza issued its findings: build two or three large dams above pool 9 and stabilize the ones that are not covered by these new dams at a cost of about $250 million. The rejected concepts were the pipeline, which was sized to serve all of central Kentucky all the time, as being too costly and the small upstream reservoirs (which had the lowest price-tag) were rejected because of the probable environmental problems associated with their construction. The Steering Committee accepted the Harza report, turned it over to the Kentucky River Authority, which was beginning to be something, and disbanded.

Lexington water has always been served by a private (for profit) company compared to municipally owned systems that are by far the most common in Kentucky. The first private company began in 1882 as the Lexington Hydraulic and Manufacturing Corporation and has evolved into the Kentucky American Water Company (KAWC). The KAWC is a wholly owned subsidiary of the American Water Works Company, Inc., a national water utility with systems all over the United States. A for-profit water company is viewed by some as a totally self-serving, maximum profit, minimum service, money grabbing organization. This is one of the problems. Another problem is that too many people wanted to get into the Lexington act and push forward their solution whether or not it had any validity. Many, many well-meaning persons have walked upon the Lexington water-problem-solving stage to play their part, and vanish. Some of these bit players wanted to keep the price of water down, always good political fodder. Other bit players said putting in water lines disturbs the earth, and some claimed that they irreversibly affect the environment like drying up springs. Many of the bit players had large audience appeal and evoked considerable applause when they said their lines.

Aside from these intangibles, however, the reality is that Lexington was located in a bad place regarding water supply. The middle of Lexington is at the beginning point of three small streams (Town Branch, Hickman Creek, and Cane Run) and has no nearby natural water source. Everything runs away from the city. The early water companies built a series of reservoirs on the southeast side of town and these served well until the drought of 1930, when they virtually dried up. A 15-mile raw water line was hurriedly built to the Kentucky River at the end of the 1930-31 drought, but it was not fully completed until after the rains came and restored the reservoirs. Since that time, however, the pumps on the Kentucky River have been the main supplier of water for Lexington, with smaller quantities from some of these reservoirs that are still in use. The old reservoirs store several days' needs, but would be quickly exhausted if not replenished from the river pumps.

Pumping from the river is limited by the withdrawal permit issued by the Division of Water. Under normal conditions, the Kentucky American Water Company (KAWC) can pump up to 63 million gallons per day from the river and has a total treatment capacity of 65 million gallons per day. This is about how much Lexington would use on a hot, dry day in 2001. When the flow in the Kentucky River is low, however, the permit cuts their withdrawal down to 30 million per day, less than half of what would be needed on a hot, dry day. In 1930 the river got this low, and it is certain it will get this low again, no one just knows when. This is the core of the "Lexington Problem": where is Lexington going to get the water that the Kentucky River cannot provide?

The KAWC knew their problem was real and would never go away. Building a bigger treatment plant was no solution as there would be no water to treat in it during a drought. The prospect of adding more storage on the Kentucky River appeared to be millions of dollars and many years away. Their eyes finally fell upon a major supply of treated water in Louisville. When Louisville was undergoing major growth and expansion in the 1970 and 80's, they built a very large water treatment plant to serve this growth. The growth in the area continued, but the service area of the Louisville Water Company was constrained and Louisville was left with about 100 million gallons per day of water treatment capacity for which there was no market, not even on the horizon. Louisville draws its water from the Ohio River or wells in the sandy banks of this river and thereby has a virtually unlimited supply of water, even during the most severe drought. This was the answer to the Lexington Problem: build a pipeline to Louisville with a capacity of about 25 million gallons per day and bring this treated water to Lexington. The estimated cost was about $50 million. Problem solved, or so thought the Kentucky American Water Company.

In 1993 the KAWC filed the necessary papers with the Kentucky Public Service Commission (PSC) to show that it was short of water and needed a supplemental source that would be available during a drought. They based their case upon the actual flow in the river during the major historical droughts (1930 was the worst, 1953, and 1988) and the findings of various studies of the Kentucky River that showed that the river was not adequate. The case did not specifically ask the PSC for permission to build a pipeline to Louisville, but the KAWC had made their intentions plain that a pipeline was the best answer to the water shortage in the river. The route of the proposed pipeline would roughly parallel I-64 from Jefferson County, but in Woodford County it would go cross country, through some prime horse-farm land. This raised a few well-heeled eyebrows in this horse-conscious county, including a former Governor and the incumbent Attorney General, both of whom owned land in Woodford County. They could visualize their million dollar horses falling into a gaping ditch while the pipeline was under construction or a water service vehicle running down one of their noble animals.

The Attorney General, whose office, by law, is obligated to "speak for the consumer" when anything comes before the PSC that would involve a utility rate increase, weighed in heavily against a finding that the Kentucky River was inadequate. He contended that cheap crest gates on certain dams or valves in the dams would provide Lexington with enough water, provided consumers cut back on their use. The KAWC countered with a public relations campaign that included lobbying, polling, and media time. They bussed senior citizens to one of the PSC hearings to give a feeling of public support for their case.

The PSC ultimately found that the KAWC did have a raw water shortage problem and that it must remedy this situation. Since there were no plans or funds to build more storage on the Kentucky River, the KAWC took this to mean that the pipeline to Louisville was the solution to the problem. The main supply would still be the Kentucky River, with the Louisville pipeline used on an as-needed basis. The Louisville water would cost more than Kentucky River water; hence, the Louisville water would be used only when the Kentucky River was not adequate. A small amount of water would be used to keep the line filled with fresh water at all times. The Company set about designing the pipeline and making arrangements with Louisville.

All of the above negotiations were made in the glare of the public eye. No sooner was the ink dry on the order from the PSC than requests for re-hearings, more public relations campaigns on both sides, more editorials against the pipeline, more billboards, and more half-truths. The pipeline opponents cited high cost, the environment, the ills of drinking water from the Ohio River, the virtues of using less water, and excess profits by the water company really who wanted to sell water along the pipeline route, as reasons to oppose it. They unashamedly used inflammatory words like "unfettered water use" and "unrestricted water demand" during a drought to paint a picture in the mind of the audience of reckless and irresponsible water use during a drought. The water company contended that they supported water conservation and only wanted to meet the reasonable needs of their customers during a drought. The pipeline was the cheapest way to solve this problem. They also said that without the pipeline Lexington could be without water for 53 days if a 1930 drought returned. They said that they were obligated to serve water to their customers all the time, not just part of the time, and they intended to do just that. Some of what both sides said was actually true.

While this rhetoric was waxing strong, a new set of actors walked upon the Lexington stage: the Fayette County Water Supply Planning Council. The 1994 Legislature mandated that each Kentucky county establish a Water Supply Planning Council, made up of local officials and citizens, the goal of which was to produce a long range water supply plan for that county good through the year 2020. The water supply system in each Kentucky county, except Fayette, is publicly owned and is thereby sensitive to the local political environment. In Fayette County the question was: how much authority would such a Water Supply Planning Council or even the City Council have over a private water company? Also the question: is the Water Supply Planning Council under the control of the City Council or can it go its own way?

Lexington Mayor Pam Miller appointed sixteen members to this Council, three of whom were members of the Lexington-Fayette Urban County Council (City Council). The others were staff members of various city government departments, other agencies (including the KAWC), and private citizens. Their first meeting was in July 1997. This Council may be phased out in the future.

From the very early meetings of this Council it was evident that two sides were emerging: those who favored the pipeline to Louisville to make up the water shortage and those who said the Kentucky River had plenty of water, consumers just needed to use less of it during a drought. Most of the many arguments of this Council were around tangents to these sides: what will be the population of Fayette County in 2020? How much water do we really need in a drought? What is the cost of the pipeline? What is the cost of a new treatment plant? Will crest gates work? How long will it take to get new storage on the river? Where will the money come from to "fix" the river? What will happen if there is a toxic spill in the river? In general, various pressure groups and the City Council representatives favored the Kentucky River option and using less water during a drought. Also in the corner opposing the pipeline were the local newspaper, the Attorney General, several other City Council members, and other individuals. In the pipeline corner were the KAWC, the Chamber of Commerce, some City employees, and individual members of the Water Supply Planning Council. At times the discussions became heated, especially when the pressure groups brought in large numbers of their supporters. The Kentucky River Authority and the Lexington Mayor remained on the sidelines.

In July 1999 the Water Supply Planning Council voted to keep the Kentucky River as the principal water supply with the pipeline to Louisville as a backup. Representatives from the City Council who were members of the Water Supply Planning Council and had attended a few of the meetings did not show up for the vote. The City Council, as a whole, feeling the weight of the barrels of ink against any use of the pipeline and the pressure of the pressure groups upon their shoulders, cried foul and requested that the report not be forwarded to the State. The Water Supply Planning Council did not feel such weight nor the heel or the blast from the City Council and later filed the report anyway.

The City Council, wanting to flex its muscle, created itself into a water supply planning "committee" (committee of the whole) to hear and decide for itself what was best for Lexington. The Mayor was not part of these meetings. The KAWC prudently agreed to abide by the findings of the City Council. The Kentucky Water Resource Research Institute (KWRRI), a University of Kentucky water think-tank, arranged for various presentations before the City Council. It was no secret that the KWRRI opposed the pipeline and this may have been one of the reasons that they were asked to set up these meetings. During the fall of 1999 a number of meetings were held and a variety of positions presented. The KAWC presented its case for the pipeline, the pressure groups who had the ear of several City Council members presented their opposition to it, and other water experts made statements.

The findings of the City Council hinged on two key presentations: the Kentucky River Authority spokesman told them that plans were in the works to raise Lock 10 by 4', which would make nearly one billion gallons of additional storage on the Kentucky River available to Lexington. He said that if everything went smoothly, this could be done in six years at a cost of just a few million dollars. This was music floating into City Council ears. The second presentation was by the KWRRI professors. They told the City Council that the computer model they had developed showed that the Kentucky River was adequate as the Lexington water supply. More music floated into City Council ears.

There were some key points, however, that this music may have drowned out. The first was that the six year timeframe for raising lock 10 was based on everything moving at lightening speed, with no hitches. The major steps in this process were design, funding, environmental matters, land acquisition, and construction. None of these had begun at that time, and the steps not under the control of the Kentucky River Authority, like funding and environmental matters, could take several years in themselves. It was not known just when the six years would begin or if they would stretch into many more. Where were the funds to rebuild the decaying locks and dams just to hold water to come from? Many millions of somebody's dollars would be required. Who was this somebody? The second matter that the music may have drowned out was the fact that the Kentucky River was adequate only if very large draw-downs of the pools on the Kentucky River, some as much as 6-feet, could be made. This had never been done before, and there was no certainty that the Division of Water would permit such a draw-down. The third point was that the allowable Lexington withdrawal from the Kentucky River would be severely reduced, in some cases by more than one half of normal, when the draw-down of the pools was under way. This would mean that only very basic water uses would be permitted under these conditions. Virtually all uses not needed to support life would be forbidden, by force of law.

Lexington City Council members are no different from most of us; they heard what they wanted to hear, did not hear what they did not want to hear, and over-whelmly voted the Kentucky River as the sole Lexington water supply and to review the matter again in three years. As the KAWC had previously agreed to abide by the wishes of this City Council, there was a big hug-in, the lights were turned out, and everybody went home. The findings of the City Council were attached to the report of the Water Supply Planning Council when it was submitted to the State. This stage was then closed for three years as far as the City Council was concerned. The pipeline was off the table.

Even though the lights on this stage were turned off, there were still unanswered questions about the water supply for Lexington: what would Lexington do for water if the rickety, 100-year-old lock & dam #9 failed before it could be fixed, which was many years away? It had been flanked by the 1905 flood and showed distinct signs of its old age. If this dam, or any of its components failed, the Lexington intake would be high and dry above the water level. What if no funding could be found to build more storage on the Kentucky River or if new storage could not be built? Where would Lexington get water if a toxic spill happened on the Kentucky River above the intake? It had happened below the intake and could just as easily happen above it. What was Lexington to do if a major drought happened before new storage and water treatment was built? What would be the public perception of Lexington knowing that it had an inadequate water supply? These questions and more were asked upon a darkened stage.

Mother Nature, however, can dominate any stage upon which she strides and does not always follow the script. While the Fayette Water Supply Planning Council and the Lexington-Fayette Urban County Council were bickering over the pipeline to Louisville and the adequacy of the Kentucky River as the sole Lexington water supply, Mother Nature was drying up the river. Compared to the record drought of 1930, which began in early spring and lasted until the following December, the drought of 1999 would be considered moderate, did not begin until mid summer, and bottomed out in mid-late September. The amount of water that the KAWC could withdraw, however, was severely cut back. On August 27, 1999, the Mayor issued a declaration substantially limiting the use of outdoor (lawn watering, plants, etc.) water. (This declaration has the force of law with the police having authority to cite persons who water their lawns at the wrong time. While this declaration was in effect, only a handful of citations were actually issued, but one of these was to a red-faced employee of the City Planning Department, who said his automatic lawn sprinkling system came on and he did not know how to turn it off.) Most lawns survived, but many plants and shrubs died because the declaration prohib-

DROUGHT OF 1999

During the drought of the summer of 1999, Pool 9 fell below the dam crest for the first time since the 1988 drought. Normally in the summer several inches, and at times several feet, of water go over this dam crest. Pools 8 and 12 were also below the crest of their dams for about two weeks. The 1988 and 1999 droughts showed that the Kentucky River needs modification to be a reliable source of water for the municipal systems using it.

ited watering these. The water release valves in pools 12 and 13 were opened about 13'-15' to let this water pass downstream to the Lexington intake in pool 9. Pool 9 dropped to about 6' to 10' below the dam crest, as did pool 8 and pool 11. Water flowed over the crest of the other dams.

Because this drought came late in the growing season, its effects upon Lexington were not as severe as a drought in the early part of the growing season. Had these water-use-reduction been in effect in June rather than the end of August, many, and possibly most, lawns, shrubs, and gardens would have been lost. The effect of water reduction on industry and commerce is hard to measure, but water is a component in the desirability of a place to live.

The lights are now out on the Lexington Problem stage, but the Problem is far from solved. This part of the drama is not ended. The switch to these lights is now in the hands of others.

On Stage Three - On the River[3]

The lights on this stage were dimly on as the audience took its seat in the theater in 1986-87. There was nothing happening on this stage worth seeing. Nobody noticed these dim lights until they became much brighter in 1990 with the reemergence of the principal actor of this entire drama – The Kentucky River Authority.

The dim lights and bland stage until 1990 was the fact that the Kentucky River Authority was created, on paper, in 1986, but Authority members were not to be appointed until the State actually owned locks and dams #5-#14. This has not happened (except for lock #10) at this writing in early 2001. When the paper Kentucky River Authority was created, the main thought was for an independent state agency actually to own the locks and dams. Since ownership of the locks and dams was still with the Corps of Engineers, there was no need for a State Authority to exist, so it did not. The locks were operated on summer weekends under lease from the Corps by a section in the Department of Natural Resources. This seemed to be working well until the 1988 drought hit.

The 1988 drought woke many people up, including some dozing in Frankfort, for the need to enhance the Kentucky River for water supply. It instantly became plain that more work was needed on the river than opening and closing the leaky gates on summer weekends for a few pleasure boats. Major work was needed on the river and major work required major capital and a special source of funds to get it. This was not the business of the Department of Natural Resources. When the dozing heads in Frankfort became fully awake, they spotted the paper with "Kentucky River Authority" written on it. Here was the answer.

The 1990 Legislature gave the Kentucky River Authority the power to build capital projects on the Kentucky River, sell bonds to pay for these, and collect water withdrawal fees to amortize the bonds. Board members were appointed by the Governor and they began to meet. The legislation did not, however, give the Kentucky River Authority any funds to operate itself; it could hire no staff, own no equipment, incur no expenses, or pay any bills. It borrowed paper clips and writing pads from the Department of Natural Resources, under whom it was sort of a step-child.

In its step-child capacity to the Department of Natural resources, however, the Kentucky River Authority can boast of two major accomplishments: it received the Harza Report from the Scotty Baelser Lexington Steering Committee, which showed the horrible condition of the locks and dams on the Kentucky River together with a plan to fix them; and it twisted Congress' arm to release funds to stabilize the 100-year old dams before their transfer to the state. The bulky Harza Report showed that major capital was needed to fix the aging system. Previous reports itemized "dental" repair (that is filling in holes) to the locks and dams, but the Harza Report showed that much more than dental repair was needed. This made the Authority members start to eye that part of their legislation about collecting fees for water withdrawal to build major projects.

The funds that Congress released, through the Corps of Engineers that still owned all of the lock and dams, was absolutely necessary to keep the dams from washing down the river. The older ones (dams #5-#8) were of timber cribbing construction with an un-reinforced concrete cap on top of them. The timber cribbing had shifted, the concrete cap had broken into blocks, and water was pouring through the middle of the dams. The upper dams (dams #9-#14) wer e of un-reinforced concrete and in slightly better condition, but not much. The basic stabilization technique used by the Corps was to drive a line of sheet piling several feet behind (upstream) the dam and fill this space with gravel and concrete. The dams also received a new concrete cap, this time with reinforced concrete. Stabilization work has been done on dams #5 thr ough #14 at a total cost of about $15 million in four appropriations.

While the Corps was busy stabilizing the dams with the first $10 million set up by Congress, the Kentucky River Authority took a deep breath and devised a withdrawal fee schedule for all users of Kentucky River water in any form above 10,000 gallons per day except agricultural uses. A two-tiered fee schedule was established in which all users of water in the basin would pay 2.2 cents per 1000 gallons withdrawn, and mainstem users, who would likely benefit from stabilization of the lock/dam system, would pay a second tier fee of an additional 1.6 cents per thousand gallons, both of which could be passed on to the water customers. These fees meant that an average family using about 5,000 gallons per month would pay about 20 cents each month to this fee. The first tier (2.2 cents) would pay for the operation of the Authority and fund various water quality and water planning programs. The second tier could be used only to fund capital construction/maintenance projects on the main stem, meaning work on the lock/dam system that the Corps would not do. At the present time, Tier I generates about $900,000 to $1 million per year and Tier II generates about $330,000 to $350,000 per year.

Everything on the river needed repair and the water supply was still in jeopardy, but the Authority knew it could not do everything at once. The Legislation had given them bonding power of only $4 million, and that would not go very far toward repair of the aging locks and dams, much less add any new water storage to the system. In 1995 the Authority selected Harza Engineering to update the work done for Scotty Baesler's Steering Committee. In this study Harza was not bound by specific concepts as they were in their previous study, so they were able to examine any alternate for increasing the water supply. The new Harza study determined that sufficient water storage could be obtained by adding movable "crest gates" to the tops of the upstream dams (all or some of #9-#14) and installing valves in the dams to release water when its level was below the crest of these dams. This meant that the water stored in the upstream pools could be released to the downstream pools when the water was at dam-level. This was not possible without the valves. The cost of this was far less than the $250 million price tag for new major dams as their previous study called for. This was good news to the Kentucky River Authority.

Raising the crest of a dam four feet does not sound like much, unless, of course, one happens to own property that is affected by this four feet of water. Such property exists in abundance in Pools #11 and #12 (Estill County), and the livelihood of no small number of farmers is tied to such property. The Kentucky River Authority Executive Director and members of the technical staff were interviewed on a local radio talk show in Estill County to discuss the raising of Pools 11 and 12. After the interview they were greeted outside the studio by an angry group of farmers who owned the land that may be affected by the four-foot increase. Angry Estill County farmers can be very persuasive, and the concept of permanently raising the dams was shelved.

The wrath of angry Estill County farmers notwithstanding, the need for storage still existed, and the Authority looked for other techniques to get it. Because the need for storage exists only during droughts why not use movable crest gates that would be up only when a drought appears to be on the horizon. They would be taken down when rains came ending the drought and the need for storage was over. If the movable crest gates were removed before the flow in the river became large, the Estill County farms would not be affected.

The best news was, however, that the valves could be installed right away at a cost of less than $50,000 each, a mere pittance compared to the $250 million price still on the table from the first Harza report. For all practical purposes this was free water! The valves were a God-send in two ways: first, they could be installed immediately by the Corps of Engineers as part of their dam-stabilization program currently under way on the upper (#11-14) dams; secondly, there were already openings through the dams on which these valves could be installed. The openings were the result of bad engineering. Dams #9 and #10 had been "flanked," that is, washed-out-around soon after they were built, by the 1905 flood. As engineers always do when things go wrong, there was finger-pointing as to whom to blame for the disaster. These fingers generally point in circles among the engineers and contractors involved in the project, but in this case the fingers (wrongly) pointed to the fact that these two dams had been built about four feet higher than the previous ones and were therefore too high to be stable.

The real reasons they were flanked were that the dirt excavated to build the lock chamber was not compacted immediately after the completion of the lock construction, but left to "settle" for one year before placing a concrete covering (esplanade) over it and the fact that the "cutoff" walls (the underground walls perpendicular to the river on either end of the excavation area) were far too short to hold the loose dirt in place during high water. The flood of 1905 simply washed this loose dirt away leaving the lock chamber in the apparent middle of the river, with the river flowing on the land-side of the lock chamber.

To overcome to what they attributed the flanking problem, the dams above #10 were designed about four feet lower than required to create a flat pool all the way to the next upstream dam during low water. This problem was to be overcome by raising four-foot "crest gates" on top of each dam each summer to increase the water level high enough to reach the next dam upstream and lower the crest gates before the flood season the following winter. In order to raise or lower these crest gates, the pools had to be lowered below the dam crest for the work to take place. The crest gates could not be raised or lowered with water flowing over them. Very large valves, with large openings, were placed in the dams to permit the pools to be lowered twice each year for the process to take place. The movable crest gates on the dams never worked particularly well, and the dams were ultimately raised to the height of the crest gates, but the large openings through the dams were still there. It was across these openings that the slide-valves were placed by the Corps of Engineers in the late 1990's to permit upstream water to be passed downstream. This use was not in the remote dreams of the engineers who (wrongly) lowered the height of these dams after the 1905 disaster but for these openings central Kentucky is forever benefited. These valves are now fully installed and were successfully used to dampen the impact of the 1999 drought on Lexington water users.

Bill Grier

VALVE OPERATION

One of the major contributions of the Kentucky River Authority to the river system was the installation of valves in Locks 11-14. These 42-inch x 42-inch could release up to 200 cfs of water from these pools for downstream use. They were highly effective in reducing the impact of the 1999 drought to Lexington.

This photo is Chief Lockmaster Earl Gulley operating the valve at Lock 13.

The Kentucky River Authority nearly sprained its arm in patting itself on the back that something had finally been done to increase the water supply to river users, at a very small cost, but it knew that this was just the beginning of its task. Navigation in the upper pools (#11-#14) was cut off by the concrete barriers placed across the lock chambers to stabilize them when the dams were stabilized. Locks #8 and #9 had been closed to navigation because

LOCK CHAMBER BULKHEADS

Bulkheads or concrete barriers were placed across the lock chambers (on the upper sill) of locks 11, 12, 13, and 14. The top of these bulkheads was about 2-feet higher than the dam crest, which meant that during low flow when the water was less than 2-feet over the dams, these bulkheads would stop the leakage through the lock gates. They stabilized the lock walls, but also prevent use of the locks for navigation.

of failure of various parts of the lock chamber and its mechanics. In the summer of 2000, large chunks of the lock #10 wall fell off forcing the closure of this lock to navigation, much to the sorrow of the two boat clubs above and below this lock. These inconveniences were but small, however, compared to the catastrophe which constantly loomed on the horizon: the failure of a key lock or dam. Because they had been flanked and repaired after the 1905 flood, because they had obvious, major problems, and because they provided water to more people than all the rest combined, locks and dams #9 and #10 wer e the focus of this concern.

In 1999-2000 the Kentucky River Authority undertook a detailed geo-technical examination of lock #10 with the intent of stabilizing the structure, restoring navigation, and possibly adding about 4' to its height by either permanently raising it or adding crest gates. The results of the examination showed that by current dam standards the structure was not stable and the cost to do all of the things desired would be about $25 million. This was not good news. Lock #9 had not been examined like this, but the cost to stabilize and restore it would probably be about the same amount also.

The Kentucky River Authority immediately set about getting $25 million for lock #10. This was far beyond its own resources and the state is seldom inclined to fund expenditures of this size for a finite population. That leaves the Federal Government.

The benefited portion of the Kentucky River basin lies in the districts of Congressmen Hal Rogers and Ernie Fletcher. Together, and with the assistance of Senators Mitch McConnell and Jim Bunning, they placed the $25 million (in pieces of about $3-$4 million increments) in the year 2000 Corps of Engineers budget for the restoration of lock and dam #10. The funding will take place over the next five to six years. When completed, one of the fourteen aging locks and dams will be stabilized and restored. The others are still waiting and failing.

The lights and activity on this stage will remain long after those of the other stages are out and quiet. As the drama subsides, the audience will tend to drift away, but will drop by from time to time to see what is going on. There will be flurries of drama as the progress of lock and dam restoration takes place but there will also be times when the lights are on but the actors are moving sluggishly about. The potential for catastrophe is constantly looking the audience in the eye.

HIGH BRIDGE PARK PAVILION REBIRTH

The rebirth of the Kentucky River includes the renovation, or in this case the rebuilding, of historic sites along its shores. At the turn of the 20th century High Bridge Park was the center of considerable social and cultural activity for crowds from as far away as Cincinnati. In the closing years of the 20th century, it fell into total decay. The Jessamine County Fiscal Court, with the assistance of the Kentucky River Authority, have rebuilt the pavilion as well as the entire park.

Ongoing Life

To an alien from outer space, the reborn Kentucky River of today would look little different from its life of 1917, but to those who know and depend upon the river, its new life is vastly changed from its old. Rafts of logs and coal barges no longer descend its waters, nor do packet boats carry merrymakers to the circus. The wild game that is transported upon its waters is not the dried venison that would sustain a Native American family through a cold winter season but is fish flopping about in the wet-well of a sleek fishing boat. Possibly unseen by the casual outer space visitor are the municipal and industrial water intakes tucked into the coves of the river or partially obscured by overhanging branches. These are the heartbeat of the River Reborn, the giver of life to the body of the River Basin. The unseen release valves in the dams assure Lexington and all the other water users a supply of water they never had before.

Much maturity awaits its reborn life: the dam stabilization program completed, the transfer of the title to Kentucky, increased storage, the repaired locks; the withdrawal fees, and much more. All of these are the growing pains of a living body. Maturity never comes easily. The Kentucky River Authority will endure the perils of childhood, the temptations of youth, and the responsibilities of adulthood.

Engineer Welsh never dreamed that his pools would be the lifegiver to cities far from the shores of the river that he wished to make into a commercial highway. His hopes of barges lining the river were never realized, but the impact of his pools upon the prosperity of central Kentucky is far greater than his wildest imagination would permit.

MAJOR QUOTATION SOURCES AND OTHER SOURCE NOTES

Life One – The Native Years
1.   Lewis, R. Barry, Editor: *Kentucky Archaeology*, 17

Life Two – Flatboats and Keelboats to the Dawn of Steam
1.   Verhoeff, Mary, *The Kentucky River Navigation*, 56
2.   Verhoeff, Mary, *The Kentucky River Navigation*, 57
3.   Verhoeff, Mary, *The Kentucky River Navigation*, 224
4.   Verhoeff, Mary, *The Kentucky River Navigation*, 226
5.   Shreve, Royal Oran:, *The Finished Scoundrel*, 294
6.   Verhoeff, Mary, *The Kentucky River Navigation*, 66
7.   Verhoeff, Mary, *The Kentucky River Navigation*, 222
8.   Verhoeff, Mary, *The Kentucky River Navigation*, 47
9.   Verhoeff, Mary, *The Kentucky River Navigation*, 85
10. Verhoeff, Mary, *The Kentucky River Navigation*, 86
11. Allen, Michael, *Western Rivermen, 1763-1861*, 56
12. Verhoeff, Mary, *The Kentucky River Navigation*, 50
13. Verhoeff, Mary, *The Kentucky River Navigation*, 134
14. Verhoeff, Mary, *The Kentucky River Navigation*, 150
15. Verhoeff, Mary, *The Kentucky River Navigation*, 156
16. Verhoeff, Mary, *The Kentucky River Navigation*, 156
17. Verhoeff, Mary, *The Kentucky River Navigation*, 163
18. Verhoeff, Mary, *The Kentucky River Navigation*, 174
19. Verhoeff, Mary, *The Kentucky River Navigation*, 179
20. Verhoeff, Mary, *The Kentucky River Navigation*, 95
21. Hunter, Louis C.: *Steamboats on the Western Waters*, 10
22. Verhoeff, Mary, *The Kentucky River Navigation*, 97
23. Coleman, J. Winston Jr., *Steamboats on the Kentucky River*, 11
24. Glenn, Nettie Henry; *Early Frankfort Kentucky - 1786-1861*, 2
25. Johnson, Leland, Correspondence to Jerry Raisor, 1997

Life Three – The Golden Age of Locks and Dams
1.   Johnson, Leland R.: *The Falls City Engineers, A History of the Louisville District Corps of Engineers - 1970-1983*, 244
2.   Verhoeff, Mary, *The Kentucky River Navigation*, 27-28
3.   Verhoeff, Mary, *The Kentucky River Navigation*, 103

4. Verhoeff, Mary, *The Kentucky River Navigation*, 30-31
5. Coleman, J. Winston Jr., *Steamboats on the Kentucky River*, 16
6. Coleman, J. Winston Jr., *Steamboats on the Kentucky River*, 17
7. Verhoeff, Mary, *The Kentucky River Navigation*, 218-221
8. Johnson, Leland R.: *The Falls City Engineers, A History of the Louisville District Corps of Engineers - 1970-1983*, 251
9. S&D Reflector: *Going to the Circus, Kentucky River Travel in 1886*; June 1996, Page 31;
10. Corps of Engineers, Annual Reports for years indicated.
11. Johnson, Leland R.: *The Falls City Engineers, A History of the Louisville District Corps of Engineers - 1970-1983*, 265
12. Bryant, Betty: *Here Comes the Showboat!*, 157
13. Donaldson, Captain John, Interview 1994

Life Four – Decay and Decline

1. The river activity (tonnage, value, passengers, etc) in this chapter is taken from the Corps of Engineers Annual Reports for the respective years.
2. Donaldson, Captain John, Interview 1994
3. Donaldson, Captain John, Interview 1994
4. Donaldson, Captain John, Interview 1994
5. Walters, Lockmaster John A., Lock 10 1943 Logbook, 33
6. Corps of Engineers, 1938 Annual Report
7. Corps of Engineers, 1947 Annual Report
8. Corps of Engineers, 1960-1969 Annual Reports
9. Gulley, Lockmaster Earl, Personal Conversation with, 1998
10. Kentucky Revised Statutes, Chapter 151, HB 699, Acts of the 1986 General Assembly, Chapter 383

Life Five – The River Reborn

1. The information in this Section is taken from the Author's personal files. He was an active participant in all the activities described in this Section.
2. The information in this Section is taken from the Minutes of the various organizations described in this Section and from the Author's personal files. He was an active participant in all the activities described in this Section.
3. The information in this Section is taken from the Minutes of the Kentucky River Authority meetings and from the Author's personal files. He is a Technical Consultant to the Kentucky River Authority and was an active participant in the activities of the Authority described in this Section.

BIBLIOGRAPHY

Allen, Michael: *Western Rivermen, 1763-1861;* Louisana State University Press, Baton Rouge 70803, 1990.

American Canal Society: *A Bicentennial Inventory of America's Historic Canal Resources,* Part 4, May 1988, Freemansburg PA.

Bryant, Betty: *Here Comes the Showboat!,* University Press of Kentucky; Lexington, Kentucky, 1994.

Bunch, Clyde, *Personal conversations.* Jessamine County KY 2000

Clark, Thomas D.: *The Kentucky,* Lexington 1992 Edition.

Coleman, Winston J., Jr.; *Kentucky A Pictorial History*; The University Press of Kentucky; Lexington KY 1971.

Coleman, J. Winston Jr.: *Steamboats on the Kentucky River*; Winburn Press, Lexington KY; 1960.

Cooperative Agreement between The Kentucky River Authority and U.S. Army Corps of Engineers

Corps of Engineers, *Correspondence between the Corps of Engineers, Kentucky River Authority, and the State of Kentucky collected by Gerard J. Edelen, PE, involving the Kentucky River Locks and Dams to the Kentucky River Authority.* Packet dated August 3, 2000.

Curry, Howard: *High Bridge, A Pictorial History.* Lexington 1983.

Dean, George W., Paper on *Jessamine County Ferries,* Nicholasville KY 1997.

Donaldson, Captain John: Personal Conversations, Lexington KY 1990-1997.

Fayette County Water Supply Planning Council, *Fayette County 20 year Comprehensive Water Supply Plan,* Lexington KY, July 1999.

Fayette County Water Supply Planning Council, *Minutes of all meetings,* Lexington KY 1997-2000.

Glenn, Nettie Henry; *Early Frankfort Kentucky - 1786-1861*; 1986.

Harza Engineering Company, *Long Range Water Supply Planning Study for the Kentuky River Basin,* Chicago IL, 1991.

Henderson, A. Gwynn: Personal Conversation, Lexington KY, 1997.

Henderson, A. Gwynn and Sharp, William E.: *Mute Stones Speak Archaic Lifeways of the Escarpment Region in Jackson County, Kentucky ;* Kentucky Heritage Council; 1997.

Hunter, Louis C.: *Steamboats on the Western Waters.* Dover Publications, New York; 1977.

Johnson, Leland R.: *The Falls City Engineers, A History of the Louisville District Corps of Engineers - 1970-1983,* Louisville 1984.

Kleber, John E., Editor: *The Kentucky Encyclopedia,* The University Press of Kentucky; Lexington, Kentucky; 1992.

Kentucky Explorer, *Various Issues*, Jackson, KY;

Kentucky Legislative Research Commission: *Chronology of the Kentucky River Task Force.* Frankfort 1990.

Kentucky Legislature: *House Bill 375*; 1996 Session

Kentucky Public Service Commission, *Files on Case No. 93-434 An Investigation of the Source of Supply and Future Demand of Kentucky American Water Company*, Frankfort KY.

Kentucky River Authority: *1995 Annual Report.* Frankfort 1996.

Kentucky River Authority, *Minutes of meetings, 1990-2000,* Frankfort KY.

Kentucky River Basin Steering Committee, *Minutes of meetings 1989-1991*, Lexington KY 1991.

Kentucky Water Resources Research Institute: *Evaluation of Water Supply in the Kentucky River Basin.* Lexington 1996.

Lewis, R. Barry, Editor: *Kentucky Archaeology,* University Press of Kentucky, Lexington Kentucky; 1997.

Lexington Herald-Leader, *Various articles, columns, and editorials,* Lexington KY 1997-2000.

Memorandum of Understanding between the Unites States Army Corps of Engineers and the Commonwealth of Kentucky; dated 22 February 1985 with Supplement dated 14 October 1988.

Parrish, Charles E., *Personal conversations with*

Parrish, Charles E. *Video Taped talk to "Historic Frankfort, Inc." in October 1995*

Parrish, Charles E.: *History of Navigation on the Kentucky River*: The Army Engineer, March-April 1995.

Pollack, David; Munson, Cheryl Ann; Henderson, A. Gwynn*: Slack Farm and the Carbon-Welburn People*; Kentucky Archaeological Survey; Lexington KY; 1996.

Boating Guide: *Kentucky River Cruise*; Published by: The Waterways Journal. St. Louis 1989.

O'Malley, Nancy O.: *Searching for Boonsborough;* Archaeological Report 193, Kentucky Anthropological Research Facility, Lexington KY 1990.

S&D Reflector: *Going to the Circus, Kentucky River Travel in 1886*; June 1996, Page 31; Published by Sons and Daughters of Pioneer River Men.

Shreve, Royal Oran: *The Finished Scoundrel* (Biography of General James Wilkinson); Bobbs-Merill Company, Indinapolis, 1933.

The Kentucky River Steering Committee: *Final Meeting Minutes*; August 28, 1991. Lexington 1991.

U. S. Army Corps of Engineers: *Kentucky River Locks and Dams* A Pamphlet, undated.

U. S. Army Corps of Engineers: *Kentucky River Navigation Charts*; January 1942 and June 1978, Louisville.

U. S. Army Corps of Engineers *Annual Reports*, Beginning 1885

U. S. Army Corps of Engineers, *Drawings on Kentucky River Locks and Dams,* Louisville KY, Beginning 1880 .

Ulack, Richard, Editor in Chief; *Atlas of Kentucky*: The University Press of Kentucky; Lexington KY; 1998.

United States Claims Court: *Civil Action 91-1516-C;* Commonwealth of Kentucky ET AL vs. United States of America.

United States District Court, Eastern District of Kentucky, Frankfort: *Civil Action 89-77*: Commonwealth of Kentucky ET AL vs. U.S. Army Corps of Engineers.

Verhoeff, Mary; *The Kentucky River Navigation;* Filson Club Publication No. 28; John. P. Morton & Company; Louisville KY; 1917.